PRIMA'S Official Strategy Guide

StarCraft™

W9-BNC-586

by Bart Farkas

Prima Publishing
Rocklin, California
(916) 632-4400
www.primagames.com

StarCraft | Prima's Official Strategy Guide

is a registered trademark of Prima Publishing,
a division of Prima Communications, Inc.

and Prima Publishing® are registered
trademarks of Prima Communications, Inc.

Project Editor: Sara E. Wilson

ISBN: 7615-0496-6
Library of Congress Catalog Card Number: 97-69508
Printed in the United States of America

01 DD 2827

For Cori,

who moves me

in more ways than one.

Acknowledgments

There are so many people to thank I almost don't know where to start. First, I'd like to say that the experience of working at Blizzard while writing this book was exceptional. The Blizzard team provided me with every last bit of support I needed, and they did it in a pleasant and professional manner. Every person at the Blizzard offices should take a bow!

Several Blizzard employees not only helped me with the strategies and *StarCraft* learning curve, but also put up with my plethora of bad jokes as the nights wore on. To Eric Dodds, Jamie Wiggs, Judah Mehler, Derek Simmons, Frank Gilson, John Lagrave, Ted Barken, Alen Lapidis, Kirk Mahony, Mike Brannigan, Chris Sigaty, and Brian Love I say a *huge* thank you. These guys all contributed to this book in one way or another, so as you read along, sit back and imagine John Lagrave telling me for the twenty-third time that if I don't build Sunken Colonies along the ridge the Protoss will wax me.

Thanks also must go out to Bill Roper at Blizzard, who helped make this book happen. I appreciated his expertise and pleasant manner. And the crew at Prima— what can I say? To Sara Wilson and Amy Raynor I simply say "Thanks" for putting up with "Mr. Grumpy" during the crunch period. Sara deserves a medal for putting up with my panicky phone calls regarding the difficulty of Protoss 10! Finally, I'd like to thank Jeff Govier, who contributed greatly to the multiplayer chapter and helped hold down the farm while I was away—thanks, man!

CONTENTS

CHAPTER 1: How to Use This Book

A Great Game . . . 2
Strategy . . . 2
Tables . . . 4
Cheats . . . 4

CHAPTER 2: The Inside Scoop

The Terran Force . . . 8
✳ Ground Units . . . 8
✳ Air Units . . . 19
✳ Terran Structures . . . 25

The Zerg Force . . . 26
✳ Ground Units . . . 26
✳ Air Units . . . 38
✳ Zerg Structures . . . 45

The Protoss Force . . . 46
✳ Ground Units . . . 46
✳ Air Units . . . 54
✳ Protoss Structures . . . 61

CHAPTER 3: General Strategy

The Terrans . . . 65
✳ General Strategies and Tips . . . 66
✳ Against the Zerg . . . 67
✳ Against the Protoss . . . 68

The Zerg . . . 69
✳ General Strategies and Tips . . . 70
✳ Against the Terrans . . . 71
✳ Against the Protoss . . . 72

The Protoss . . . 73
✳ General Strategies and Tips . . . 74
✳ Against the Terrans . . . 75
✳ Against the Zerg . . . 76

CHAPTER 4: The Terran Missions

MISSION #1:   Wasteland . . . 80

MISSION #2:   Backwater Station . . . 83

MISSION #3:   Desperate Alliance . . . 87

MISSION #4:   The Jacobs Installation . . . 91

MISSION #5:   Revolution . . . 94

MISSION #6:   *Norad II* . . . 99

MISSION #7:   The Trump Card . . . 104

MISSION #8:   The Big Push . . . 108

MISSION #9:   New Gettysberg . . . 113

MISSION #10:   The Hammer Falls . . . 118

CHAPTER 5: The Zerg Missions

MISSION #1:   Among the Ruins . . . 124

MISSION #2:   Egression . . . 128

MISSION #3:   The New Dominion . . . 132

MISSION #4:   Agent of the Swarm . . . 135

MISSION #5:   The Amerigo . . . 139

MISSION #6:   The Dark Templar . . . 142

MISSION #7:   The Culling . . . 146

MISSION #8:   Eye for an Eye . . . 151

MISSION #9:   The Invasion of Aiur . . . 156

MISSION #10:   Full Circle . . . 161

CHAPTER 6: The Protoss Missions

MISSION #1:   First Strike . . . 166

MISSION #2:   Into the Flames . . . 169

MISSION #3:   Higher Ground . . . 173

MISSION #4:   The Hunt for Tassadar . . . 177

MISSION #5:   Choosing Sides . . . 181

MISSION #6:   Into the Darkness . . . 185

MISSION #7:   Homeland . . . 189

MISSION #8:   The Trial of Tassadar . . . 194

MISSION #9:   Shadow Hunters . . . 199

MISSION #10:   Eye of the Storm . . . 203

CHAPTER 7: Multiplayer Games

Battle.net . . . 210
* Updates . . . 210
* Troubleshooting . . . 211
* Is the Connection Good? . . . 211

The Multiplayer Experience . . . 212
* The Human Factor . . . 212

Multiplayer Tips . . . 213
* Speed . . . 213
* Keep Your Scan Going . . . 213
* Defending . . . 214
* Attacking . . . 215

CHAPTER 8: Campaign Editor

What Is It? . . . 218
Building Your Own Map . . . 219
Experiment! . . . 227

APPENDIX A: Unit Tables

Terran Unit Table . . . 230
Zerg Unit Table . . . 231
Protoss Unit Table . . . 232
Terran Structures . . . 233
Zerg Structures . . . 234
Protoss Structures . . . 235
Hero Statistics . . . 236
Terran Counter Table . . . 237
Zerg Counter Table . . . 238
Protoss Counter Table . . . 239

APPENDIX B: Tech Trees

Terran Unit Dependencies . . . 240
Zerg Unit Dependencies . . . 241
Protoss Unit Dependencies . . . 242
Terran Building Dependencies . . . 243
Zerg Building Dependencies . . . 244
Protoss Building Dependencies . . . 245

APPENDIX C: Cheat Codes

Cheat Codes . . . 246

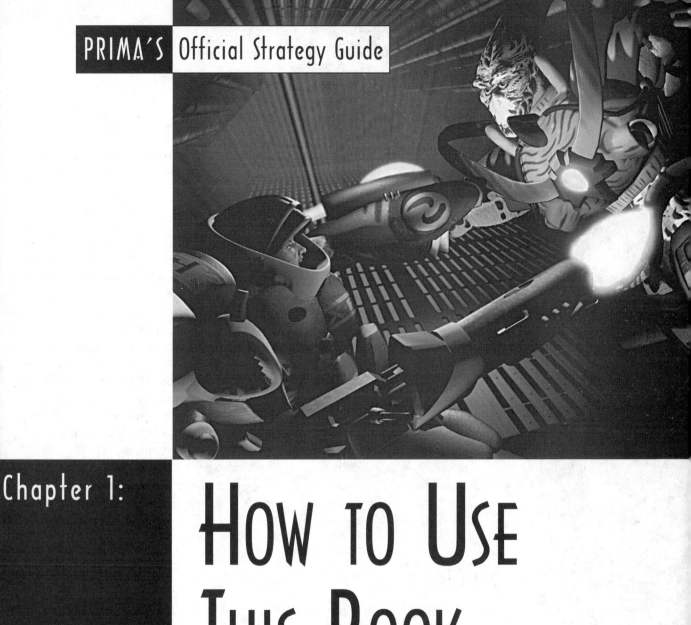

Chapter 1:

How to Use
This Book

A Great Game

*S*tarCraft is an awesome game, one that hundreds of thousands (if not millions) of gamers will play in years to come. It's a truly compelling strategic adventure pulled together by a team of skilled programmers, writers, artists, musicians, and testers at the Blizzard offices in Irvine, California. Blizzard, for those who are not aware of the incredible accomplishments of this company, has had a string of unprecedented hits over the past few years. Beginning with *WarCraft*™, Blizzard has single-handedly become the crown prince of the strategy game genre, and with their subsequent releases of *WarCraft*™ II, *WarCraft II* Expansion Pack, and the ground-breaking *Diablo*™ Blizzard has arguably become the number one computer game producer of the 1990s.

Although *StarCraft* appears to be a logical extension of the *WarCraft* series of games, it's actually leaps and bounds ahead of its predecessors in many ways. Sure, the graphics and animation are considerably tighter and more defined, and the cutscenes in *StarCraft* are absolutely beyond belief, but those aren't the only areas where *StarCraft* distinguishes itself. Indeed, *StarCraft* truly shines because it is simple to learn, and yet complex when it comes to mounting successful strategies. For the hoards of *WarCraft* and *WarCraft II* fans, *StarCraft* continues the lineage in a grand fashion by providing a gaming experience that far exceeds its ancestors.

Because *StarCraft* is such a compelling and complex game, this book will be a handy reference long after you've finished the final battle. Great games like this live a long and fruitful life, and this strategy guide will help you with major and minor details along the way.

Strategy

StarCraft's complexity inspires almost as many different strategies as it has players, so it's safe to assume you'll find ways to defeat a scenario that differ from these. That's OK. If you follow this book's guidance for each scenario, you'll win, but this guidance isn't the be-all and end-all. Rather, it's distilled from tried-and-true methods of defeating each and every mission.

I recommend you attempt to defeat each scenario by yourself first—give it at least a couple of tries—before you turn to this book's strategies. To maximize your fun, use these strategies only when you absolutely have to. Finding your own ways to defeat the tougher *StarCraft* scenarios is well worth the effort. If frustration sets in, however, this book is here for you.

Chapter Two, the background information chapter, is chock-full of strategies and tips for each individual unit in every race. To learn what each unit can do, it will serve you well to read this chapter end to end. As a bonus, we include detailed tables outlining statistics for each unit and structure, and provide the inside scoop on *StarCraft*'s heroes.

Chapter Three is meant to be used in conjunction with Chapter Two, helping you to meld the individual unit strategies in with the overall tips and strategies supplied in Chapter Three. Many of the tips and tricks supplied in Chapter Three came straight from the fine folks at the Blizzard testing department, thereby giving you access to the most experienced *StarCraft* gamers in the world. Heed the advice in Chapter Three, it will serve you well in the months ahead.

In chapters Four, Five, and Six you'll find the individual detailed strategies for defeating each of the scenarios. It's probably best if you only refer to this section of the book when you really need the help, because if you read up on each strategy before you begin the mission it'll take away some of the magic that *StarCraft* is intended to provide. Rather than using it as a walkthrough, use the individual mission strategies when you're really stuck or after you've successfully finished a mission. You'll be surprised at how often your strategy differs from the one in this book, which is proof of the fantastic complexity of *StarCraft*.

Chapter Seven endeavors to give you some help with setting up a multiplayer game, as well as strategies and tips for surviving in the cutthroat world of mano-a-mano and group *StarCraft* gaming. Multiplayer action is where the legacy of *StarCraft* will truly live on, and if you love the game as much as most people do, you'll be eager to get online and learn the skills to succeed in the Battle.net realm.

As if *StarCraft* and its Multiplayer action isn't enough, the folks at Blizzard have also included a Campaign Editor on the *StarCraft* CD. This handy tool allows you to create your own, entirely new campaigns for *StarCraft* complete with everything except cutscenes. We grabbed a couple of Blizzard employees to walk us through the initial process of designing a scenario with the Campaign Editor, thereby giving you a starting point into your own *StarCraft* world.

Take as much or as little as you require. Scan the tables, read up on unit strategies, or just peruse the walkthroughs when you get frustrated—whatever you need to help you get the most out of *StarCraft*.

Tables

The appendix provides detailed tables with gobs of statistical information for each unit and structure. A "counter table" supplies a reasonable opposing unit from each of the other two races. For example, what Zerg unit best counters the Marine? This information may seem mundane at first, but one you've mastered *StarCraft*'s nuances you'll find even the small details can give you an edge over the computer AI or human opponent.

Cheats

Like *WarCraft* and *WarCraft II*, *StarCraft* does allow you certain latitudes when it comes to cheating. In fact, you have the same powers over the units of *StarCraft* as you did in *WarCraft II*. You can kill units, make units, build faster, get cash, move from level to level, view movies, and even get the entire tech tree built in the blink of an eye. But even though we're giving you these cheats (see Appendix C), they should come with fair warning: Don't use them until *after* you've finished the game on your own. If you use the cheats to help you win certain missions, you'll only be denying yourself some of the fun of the game. Besides, a level that was won with cheats won't let you proceed to the next level (unless you cheat to get there, too). At any rate, these cheats can be a lot of fun, so whenever you actually choose to use them, enjoy them.

Chapter 2:

THE
INSIDE
SCOOP

In this chapter you'll find detailed statistics about each unit. The tables in Appendix A supply further details, including ground and air attack values and unit counters for each race. Although this chapter covers much of this, it also contains information that will help you understand each unit's strengths and weaknesses and how the units relate as you progress through the game.

The Terran Force

The Terrans should hold a special place in your heart, if for no other reason than that they are our humanoid cousins. If you play the game through from start to finish, your first 10 missions will be Terran-controlled and will give you a solid understanding of the mechanics and strategies you need to survive in *StarCraft*. For this reason, you should play from start to finish—Terrans first, then Zerg, and finally Protoss.

Terran units are no less potent than those of the other two races. Indeed, many game testers at Blizzard prefer the Terrans, with their cloaked Wraiths and mammoth Battlecruisers packing Yamato Guns. Handled properly, the Terrans are a formidable force.

Ground Units

These units will fight the enemy on his own turf, paving the way to victory with the opponent's blood. You may be tempted to spend resources building flashy spaceships, but sometimes a group of inexpensive Marines can serve just as well.

MARINE

Armor: Light
Hit Points: 40
Ground Attack: 6
Air Attack: 6
Attack Range: 4
Gas Required: 0
Minerals Required: 50

The Marine is your bread-and-butter unit. Equally effective against both air and ground attacks, this versatile unit has been the deciding factor in many missions. The Marines often back up Wraiths or Battlecruisers because of their powerful ability to mop up nagging ground-based air defense systems while their airborne counterparts clean out the skies.

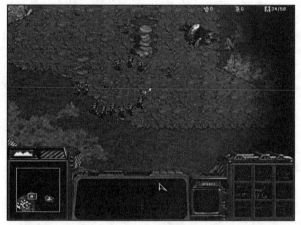

Fig. 2-1:

The Terrans' most versatile units, Marines can rock and roll both on the ground and against airborne enemies.

Groups of Marine can take down small and medium-sized squadrons of light airships quickly with their rifles. Consider the Marine an alternative to the Missile Turret whenever and wherever building one is prohibitive. You can use Marines as mobile "Missile Turrets" and deal a heavy blow to ground and air units alike; the only proviso is that they must travel in groups of eight or more.

Fig. 2-2:

Defensive Marines in Bunkers are difficult to beat.

Although the Marines can take a decent fight to enemy units, on the ground they really shine when they're stacked four at a time in a Bunker. This is especially true in the Zerg levels where the Terran bases are hit with wave after wave of Zerglings and Hydralisks. A Bunker full of Marines with extended range and beefed-up attack values can mow down the enemy indefinitely if the enemy attacks in small groups. A grid of Bunkers is virtually impenetrable.

FIREBAT

Armor: Light

Hit Points: 50

Ground Attack: 16*

Air Attack: 0

Attack Range: 2

Gas Required: 25

Minerals Required: 50

Attack value limited against some units (see Appendix A)

Their limited range and lack of an air attack give Firebats a more defined role than that of the Marines. Firebats cost more, as well (requiring Vespene). However, they have value in many Terran missions and can be instrumental in winning several battles against the Zerg.

Fig. 2-3:

Firebats and Zerglings—a good combination if you're Terran.

The Firebat is essentially a flamethrower and carries a threefold attack advantage over the Marine. This can be deceptive, however, because attacking heavy armor can lower the Firebat's attack value by 75 percent. An attack value of 16 doesn't look so good reduced to 4. What's the answer? Use the Firebat when you can take the greatest advantage of its weapons.

Firebats are *very* effective against hoards of Zerglings, particularly from the protection of a Bunker. A combination of Marines (for their attack range) and Firebats (for their raw power) in a series of defensive Bunkers will smoke Zerglings and Hydralisks (pardon the pun). Terran Mission 6, "*Norad II*" and Terran Mission 3, "Desperate Alliance," are excellent opportunities to demonstrate this.

Fig. 2-4:

This Firebat/Marine circling technique works well in the early Terran missions.

Firebat groups are also excellent for destroying enemy buildings/structures. A posse of eight to 12 Firebats circling an enemy building will incinerate it in seconds. A popular strategy (see Mission 2, "Backwater Station") is to use equal groups of Firebats and Marines as a one-two punch against enemy forces. Firebats are also very effective against Protoss Zealots units, because they must attack hand-to-hand and are vulnerable to fire due to their light armor.

GHOST

Armor: Light

Hit Points: 45

Ground Attack: 10*

Air Attack: 10*

Attack Range: 6

Gas Required: 75

Minerals Required: 25

*Attack value limited against some units (see Appendix A).

Because of its light armor, relatively low hit points, and unique skills, you won't usually produce Ghosts in bulk. However, the Ghost is one of the game's most important units, especially if you're fond of nuclear weaponry.

The Ghost's most versatile feature is its Cloak; usually you must research it to gain access to it. The Cloak is a special ability that makes it impossible for most enemy units to see the Ghost. This often leaves the Ghost free to wander deep into enemy territory to scout or paint a target for a Nuke. The Cloak isn't without drawbacks, however: Detector units such as Observers and Missile Turrets can spot cloaked Ghosts and enable other units to open fire on them.

Fig. 2-5:

The cloaked Ghost is a powerful tool if you use caution around detector units.

Lockdown is another ability unique to the Ghost. This special missile temporarily immobilizes mechanized units. Of course, this doesn't do much good against the Zerg, but you'll have plenty of opportunities to use the Lockdown in the course of playing *StarCraft*. Lockdown comes in handy if an enemy Siege Tank or Battlecruiser is giving your base trouble; just "lock it down" and take it out.

The last and best feature of the Ghost is its ability to "paint" an enemy target for a nuclear strike. Once the target is painted, a red laser-sighting dot is displayed, and after about 10 seconds, the Nuke will drop. *Boom.* The Ghost is the only unit able to do this, and sadly is often lost in the blast. The resulting damage is worth it, however. A Nuke will do substantial (if not terminal) damage to all units and structures within a large radius.

Fig. 2-6:

When a Nuke goes off, you'll know it.

GOLIATH

Armor: Heavy
Hit Points: 125
Ground Attack: 10
Air Attack: 20*
Attack Range: 5
Gas Required: 50
Minerals Required: 100

Attack value limited against some units (see Appendix A).

The Goliath is the cream of your infantry, striking fear in the hearts of the enemy. The Goliath is impressive because it has a powerful ground attack and an even more devastating air defense system. En masse, Goliaths can knock any enemy unit from the sky in seconds and are as formidable as Marines on the ground.

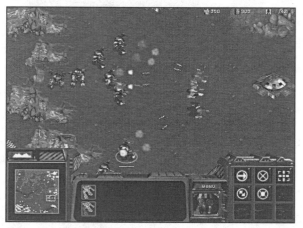

Fig. 2-7:

The Goliath's ability to take out air units is perhaps its greatest advantage.

Goliaths can provide ground support for Marines or Firebats, but, more importantly, they provide a high-powered air defense system 25 percent more potent than the Wraith's air-to-air attack! Twelve Marines backed up with four to six Goliaths are a force to reckon with when they advance on enemy positions.

Fig. 2-8:

Surprisingly, Zerglings can pose a bit of a problem for an isolated Goliath.

The Goliath's bulk renders it vulnerable to attacks by swarming enemies such as Zerglings. One or two Goliaths against a group of ten Zerglings are in trouble. When possible, always protect your units by grouping two kinds together, such as Firebats and Marines, or Marines and Goliaths.

SCV

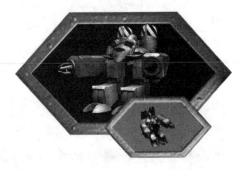

Armor: Light

Hit Points: 60

Ground Attack: 5

Air Attack: 0

Attack Range: 1

Gas Required: 0

Minerals Required: 50

The SCV looks like it might make a good fighting unit. However, the SCV doesn't really mix it up well, and you should use this unit for combat only in emergency situations. Having the SCV harvest gas and minerals is a far, far more efficient use of the resources it took to build the unit.

Fig. 2-9:

SCVs are for building structures and harvesting resources. Try not to get into this situation.

If it happens that the SCV is the only line of defense for your base, form the SCVs into a large group and throw them at the enemy en masse. This might be your only chance until you build some more effective fighting units.

Although it's a poor fighter, keep an SCV hanging around just behind the front lines so it can scoot in and repair damaged Goliaths or Siege Tanks (or even air units) when the going gets tough. This is easy to forget, but bringing a damaged unit back from the brink with an SCV is *a lot* cheaper than building another.

SIEGE TANK

Armor: Heavy

Hit Points: 150

Ground Attack (Tank):   30*

Ground Attack (Siege):   70*

Air Attack: 0

Attack Range (Siege):   12

Attack Range (Tank):   6

Gas Required :   100

Minerals Required: 150

*Attack value limited against some units (see Appendix A).

The ability to convert to Siege Mode and fire high-powered shells farther than any other unit in the game makes the Siege Tank perhaps the Terrans' most popular (and awesome) unit. However, the Siege Tank is vulnerable to air attacks and attacks by large numbers of ground units.

Fig. 2-10:

As a tank this unit deals good damage, but it really shines in a different mode.

The Siege Tank offers a good combination of mobility and firepower in combat situations. In fact, when your troops are moving so fast that you don't bother to pause to regroup, leaving your Siege Tanks in Tank Mode is probably a good idea. Otherwise they can fall behind the protective envelope of your supporting troops and become open to attack.

Fig. 2-11:

Siege Mode rules. A row of Siege Tanks can lay waste to vast numbers of advancing enemy units and, in conjunction with a Bunker, are dynamite.

As soon as you've researched Siege Mode, your tank strategy will change dramatically. The Siege Tank has an explosive attack strength of 70 and a range of 12 (the game's highest). These two values combine to provide exceptional power you can use to level enemy bases in minutes. By moving up your forces in groups of Marines, Wraiths, and Siege Tanks (in Siege Mode), with each group of units protecting the others, you can advance on the enemy at will.

NOTE Siege Tanks in Siege Mode cannot move! Also, they have a minimum range, so they are vulnerable to hand to hand attacks.

VULTURE

Armor: Medium

Hit Points: 80

Ground Attack: 20*

Air Attack: 0

Attack Range: 5

Gas Required: 0

Minerals Required: 75

Attack value limited against some units (see Appendix A).

The Vulture holds a special place in *StarCraft* because it's the vehicle of choice for Jim Raynor, one of the game's main characters. His Vulture, however, is a souped-up version of the normal craft and isn't representative of the Vulture as a unit. The Vulture is a hovercycle that's fast, powerful, and very effective when quick response time is critical.

Fig. 2-12:

Raynor's Vulture isn't your typical unit. Remember that when you're ordering up 12 of them.

The Vulture uses Fragmentation Grenades as its primary weapon and, although they pack a decent punch, their effectiveness is diminished against heavily armored enemies. The Vulture's speed is its greatest asset, because it can travel quickly from hot spot to hot spot in groups of three or four. This method of putting out fires can be very effective, especially when you're defending a sprawling base from intermittent attacks.

Fig. 2-13:

A few carefully laid Spider Mines can provide both first-line defense and an early warning system.

The Vulture's special weapon is the Spider Mine. These little devices are very effective as both defensive units and an early warning system. You must research Spider Mines, and when you get them, there are only three mines per Vulture. However, its power makes the Spider Mine worthwhile. After you set a Spider Mine, it burrows into the ground and waits for an enemy unit to get close. When it senses an enemy within its strike zone, it emerges and runs (quickly) at the enemy unit. The resulting explosion will usually take out the enemy unit and severely damage any others nearby.

MISSILE TURRET

> Armor: Heavy
>
> Hit Points: 200
>
> Ground Attack: 0
>
> Air Attack: 20*
>
> Attack Range: 7
>
> Gas Required: 0
>
> Minerals Required: 100

Attack value limited against some units (see Appendix A).

There are two important things to remember about Missile Turrets:

1. They're detectors, so they can spot cloaked enemy ships.

2. They work much, much better in groups.

With that in mind, you should build your Missile Turrets in groups of at least three, and place one anywhere you're at risk from cloaked enemies.

Fig. 2-14:

Turrets like to be grouped; otherwise they get lonely— and dead.

Keeping an SCV around to repair a damaged Missile Turret can save you rebuilding costs. Often the enemy will attack Missile Turrets in force one at a time, making the Missile Turrets difficult to keep. But an SCV on the backside usually can repair the unit quickly and save it from destruction while your other forces take care of the invaders.

Air Units

Terran air units are an impressive group featuring maneuverability, cloaking, high-powered weapons, and special abilities. Together, these features make a dangerous combination.

WRAITH

Armor: Heavy

Hit Points: 120

Ground Attack: 8

Air Attack: 15*

Attack Range: 5

Gas Required: 100

Minerals Required: 200

Attack value limited against some units (see Appendix A).

The Wraith is the Terrans' base air attack unit. Used in force, it offers a viable alternative to ground-based attacks. This may not seem prohibitive, but amassing a fleet of Wraiths can drain you quickly of the Vespene you need for other purposes. Try to ensure a solid Vespene supply before you build up a fleet.

Fig. 2-15:

Wraiths are expensive, but nice to have.

The Wraith may be a basic unit, but it has the impressive ability to cloak (when researched) in battle. Of course, cloaking is of little use near enemy detector units such as Missile Turrets or Spore Colonies. But when the Wraith is hunting down enemy Transports or strafing advancing ground troops, it's usefulness is unsurpassed.

Fig. 2-16:

Cloaked Wraiths can do some very serious damage to unsuspecting enemy units.

When assaulting an enemy position, the Wraith provides excellent air cover for Marines, Siege Tanks, and even Battlecruisers. If the enemy starts throwing air units at your strike force, cloak your Wraiths and take them out. Even if a nearby detector renders its Cloak ineffective, the Wraith's covering ability is second to none in the Terran forces.

BATTLECRUISER

Armor: Heavy

Hit Points: 500

Ground Attack: 25*

Air Attack: 25*

Air/Ground Attack (Yamato Gun):   150*

Attack Range: 6

Attack Range (Yamato Gun):   10

Gas Required: 300

Minerals Required: 400

Attack value limited against some units (see Appendix A).

If you're looking for an expensive unit, put the Battlecruiser at the top of the list. It's also quite possibly the Terrans' most powerful unit, so often the cost is worth it. The Battlecruiser is usually used as a primary weapon in a larger attack force, especially if it has the Yamato Gun. The Battlecruiser can meet an early demise if left unprotected against a group of enemy air units or a large group of Missile Turrets, so always keep a couple of protective Wraiths nearby.

Fig. 2-17:

Keep some backup near your Battlecruisers. They're worth protecting.

The Yamato Gun is the Battlecruiser's special weapon. In conjunction with other Battlecruisers, the Yamato Gun can take out an entire enemy base with just a few blasts. For example, say ten Battlecruisers (all Yamato-equipped) approach a Zerg base defended by five Spore Colonies. Each of five Battlecruisers uses its Yamato Gun to take out a Spore Colony with one shot while the other five BCs hit the Hive with their Yamatos simultaneously. *Boom.* The Hive and the entire air defense network is gone in about 15 seconds.

Fig. 2-18:

A bunch of Battlecruisers with enabled Yamato Guns is truly an awesome destructive force.

Although attacking with ten Battlecruisers sounds like fun, building the fleet requires huge amounts of resources. And while you pour your resources into Battlecruisers, your base is vulnerable to enemy attack. If the enemy attacks in force when you have only two Battlecruisers, you're in trouble. The moral of the story is *don't overdo it with just one type of unit.*

SCIENCE VESSEL

Armor: Heavy

Hit Points: 200

Ground Attack: 0

Air Attack: 0

Attack Range: 8

Gas Required: 300

Minerals Required: 25

The Science Vessel isn't really an offensive weapon, but once you research all its considerable abilities it will add a great deal to your offensive and defensive powers. The Science Vessel carries a very high Vespene cost, and so usually you won't build it in quantity. However, one or two Science Vessels can turn the tide of a scenario with one of its three special abilities.

The Science Vessel's first special ability is the Defensive Matrix. It can set this special shield around any unit (except itself) for a much higher level of protection than normal armor and shield provide. When you must get units behind enemy lines, enhance a Dropship with the Defensive Matrix so it can drop cargo without getting smoked by anti-air defenses. You can also give the Defensive Matrix to a Battlecruiser or Siege Tank to protect the forward unit of an assault. Uses for this shielding are limited only by your imagination. All good things must end, however, and after a short time, so does the Defensive Matrix shield. Keeping several Science Vessels around to protect a unit continually is a common strategy, but a protected unit still takes hits, nevertheless—just very small ones.

Fig. 2-19:

A unit with a Defensive Matrix isn't invulnerable, but it's pretty darned close.

Another special ability, the Electromagnetic Pulse Shockwave, is effective only against units that use special electronics or have shielding. The EMP Shockwave removes special energy or shielding from units within its blast radius (including your own). Obviously, this has no practical application against the Zerg, who are entirely biological, but when you're facing off against the Protoss, what better way to eliminate their units' shielding? One popular way to use the EMP Shockwave is to punch a hole in enemy lines by reducing the shields of all the units in a given area, evening the playing field for an assault.

Fig. 2-20:

Irradiate is extremely useful against tightly grouped biologic units; otherwise, it can be a waste of energy.

The Science Vessels' third special ability is Irradiate. This wide-area weapon does considerable damage to all biological units and can wipe out a closely clustered group quickly. Try not to use Irradiate unless you have a terrific opportunity—say, if eight Hydralisks are clumped together just asking for it. Using Irradiate on lone units isn't usually an efficient use of Science Vessel energy, so choose your battles carefully.

DROPSHIP

Armor: Heavy

Hit Points: 150

Ground Attack: 0

Air Attack: 0

Attack Range: 0

Gas Required: 100

Minerals Required: 100

The Dropship is simply the Terrans' air transport unit. It has medium speed and no attack or defense values, and it isn't particularly well-protected with hit points. Anytime you use Dropships, you must back them up with other units. Enemy air units can destroy an exposed Dropship in no time; having even a Science Vessel as a distraction can make the difference between successfully transporting your cargo and death.

Often the best way to avoid getting your Dropships pummeled by enemy defenses is to destroy those defenses before your Dropship even arrives. In Mission 6, "Norad II," for example, it's best to use your Dropships to unload units on the periphery of enemy defenses and let your units clear out the Spore Colonies first. Once a path is cleared, your Dropships can fly in with relative ease. The bottom line—if you're carrying mission-sensitive cargo (such as Raynor), don't risk flying a Dropship into hostile territory unless it's well-protected by Wraiths.

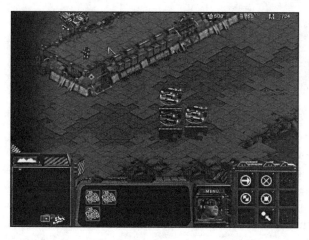

Fig. 2-21:

Dropships are vulnerable to enemy attack, so protect them well.

Terran Structures

The Terran structures have one common thing that makes them special over the other race's structures; mobility. Nearly all of the Terran units are able to pick themselves up off the ground and hover to a new location, albeit very slowly. This ability enables you to move a Barracks or a Starport from one side of the map to the other in times when you may not have the resources to build another structure. The value of being able to move your structures cannot be understated. In terms of strategy, however, the most important structures you can build are Missile Turrets and Bunkers because of their implicit defensive qualities.

BUNKERS

Bunkers, when stocked with Marines, can be used for both air and ground defense, and can even be used as an offensive weapon of sorts. It is possible to "leap frog" your Bunkers by building them closer and closer into the enemy's territory. In this way, you are establishing a defensive bulkhead over and over again as you press forward in battle.

TURRETS

Turrets, on the other hand, are used exclusively for defense—but not only for their ability to fire on air units. Turrets are also detector units, which means they can spot cloaked enemies as they approach. Often this skill is the Turret's most valuable asset, because without the detecting Turret, a base that's being attacked by an invisible attacker will eventually become rubble. Placing Turrets around bases is always a safe bet, both against air attacks and cloaked invaders as well.

THE ZERG FORCE

Now that you're fighting with the Zerg, things have changed quite a bit. First, the Zerg are a different kind of species, relying heavily on mass quantities of cheap units rather than a few superpowerful weapons. This means you must change your strategic attitudes to succeed with the Zerg.

Another important difference is that all Zerg units are biological, and as such all of them will heal themselves over time. Even a unit or structure one point from destruction can recover given time enough to recuperate. The Zerg also have a different way of building units. Rather than training or manufacturing a unit, they mutate Larvae (always squirming around the Hatchery, Lair, and Hive) into the unit they want. Drones serve a double purpose: They harvest minerals and Vespene Gas *and* they can mutate into structures. To "build" a structure, you must have a Drone to spare, because it *becomes* the structure and is lost forever.

The hierarchy of Zerg minions relates to the Overlords. Like the Terran Supply Depots and the Protoss Pylons, you need the Overlords before you can have other units in action. Each Overlord can be responsible for as many as seven units. If all your Overlords are occupied, you'll have to build more. Once you get the hang of the Zerg, you'll learn that, even though they're not as technologically advanced as the Terrans or Protoss, they're still a powerful force.

Ground Units

The Zerg are famous for their overwhelming numbers. Vast swarms of Zerglings will rip the flesh off enemy units with a zeal unknown in other races. The Zerg are bred to fight, and their ground units epitomize the ferocity programmed into them over years of genetic alteration. Using the Zerg units properly, in balanced forces, increases your chances for success in any battle.

ZERGLING

Armor:	Light
Hit Points:	35
Ground Attack:	5
Air Attack:	0
Attack Range:	0*
Gas Required:	0
Minerals Required:	50

*Must be hand-to-hand combat.

The Zergling is the base unit of the Zerg ground forces. It's a particularly vicious little creature capable of shredding a defenseless enemy to pieces in seconds. Additionally, they are cheap to produce. Fifty minerals gets you two Zerglings! This makes Zerglings ideal for quick defense should an undefended base come under attack. Just get your Hatchery to build three eggs' worth of Zerglings, and before you know it you'll have six Zerglings hopping around just dying to attack the enemy.

Fig. 2-22:

Zerglings can be a quick fix when your base is in a tight situation.

The Zerglings' supply cost also is low, accruing only half a supply point each. This makes the Zergling the perfect unit to create in bulk. It doesn't take long to create two dozen Zerglings to use in quick, swarming attacks. Zerglings are very fast, and when upgraded fully they can cover a lot of ground rapidly. They're particularly effective when used with a group of Hydralisks. The Zerglings move in and attack directly, distracting the enemy while the Hydralisks pound the opposition from afar. This technique is very effective in Zerg Mission 1, "Among the Ruins," and can be effective in subsequent missions, as well.

Fig. 2-23:

Siege Tanks can make dead Zerglings in a hurry.

The Zergling is a great weapon, but like all good things it has its limitations. The Zergling is particularly susceptible to attacks from Siege Tanks, Firebats, Carriers, and even Radiation. Basically, anything that casts a wave of destruction over a wide area is not good for Zerglings. A group of Zerglings unknowingly in range of a Siege Tank will be turned to dust before they can turn and run, so always be aware of their limitations. The Zergling, more than any other unit, has the ability to surprise, bewilder, and overwhelm an opponent.

BROODLING*

Armor: Light

Hit Points: 30

Ground Attack: 4

Air Attack: 0

Attack Range: 0***

* Broodlings are created by Queens and require energy.

** Attack value limited against some units (see Appendix A).

***Must be hand-to-hand combat.

Broodlings aren't mutated, but spawned from Queens that have learned Spawn Broodling behavior. Broodlings cause massive damage when they first hit the enemy, and then attack much like the Zerglings. A Broodling's life cycle is only as long as its energy bar. When the energy runs out, so does the Broodling.

 Spawn Broodling

This ability works as follows: The Queen targets an enemy unit (non-robotic) and uses Spawn Broodling. The target unit is destroyed and two Broodlings come into play. These are now Zerg units.

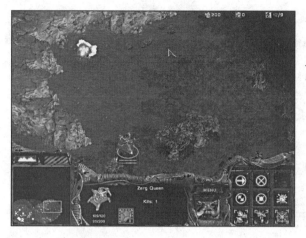

Fig. 2-24:

Once you've researched to the point where you can use Broodlings, they can come in very handy.

Broodlings are a great way to get units to places easily accessible from the air. Whether your forces on the front lines need some support or you just want to pop a few units into an enemy base to cause some chaos, the Broodling provides an easy solution. Five or six Queens can make for a pretty substantial mobile attack force for striking deep into enemy territory.

HYDRALISK

Armor:	Medium

Hit Points:	80

Ground Attack:	10*

Air Attack:	10*

Attack Range:	5

Gas Required:	25

Minerals Required:	75

*Attack value limited against some units (see Appendix A).

The Hydralisk is a core unit of any Zerg attack force. For lack of a better description, Hydralisks are a bigger, stronger Marine. This is because their attacks pack a wallop both on land and in the air, making them a versatile unit that can both attack and defend a position against nearly any enemy unit.

Fig. 2-25:

When you can keep Hydralisks in groups, they're very effective against air units.

The Hydralisk's ranged attack allows you to use it like a mobile Spore Colony that can protect other units from air attack or defend your base the same way. Generally, the Hydralisk is most effective in groups of eight or more, making it difficult for enemy units to take out any one Hydralisk before the group can take *them* out.

Fig. 2-26:

Because they're so versatile, always keep a few Hydralisks at your base.

A popular attack involves Hydralisks in one group and Zerglings in another group or two. The Zerglings will occupy enemy forces while the slower Hydralisks move into position and start their ranged attacks. This is a classic use of Hydralisks, but another effective tactic uses Hydralisks as backup for Guardians. Guardians, essentially bombers, can do major damage to ground targets, but they're incapable of firing back when attacked by air. This is where the Hydralisks come in: A group of 12 Hydralisks and 12 Guardians can move over a map together and crush enemy bases very effectively. Use the Hydralisks to blow enemy aircraft out of the sky while the Guardians concentrate on anything on the ground.

DRONE

Armor: Light

Hit Points: 40

Ground Attack: 5

Air Attack: 0

Attack Range: 5

Gas Required: 0

Minerals Required: 50

As with the SCV, you shouldn't use the Drone for attack. In a pinch, though, it has an attack capability slightly greater than that of its Terran cousin. The important thing to remember about Drones is that once they mutate into a structure they're lost forever. Their biological essence creates the new structure and is no longer available for other uses. This means you must create an extra Drone for every structure you build. Remember this; otherwise, you'll end up with lots of structures but no Drones to harvest minerals and Vespene.

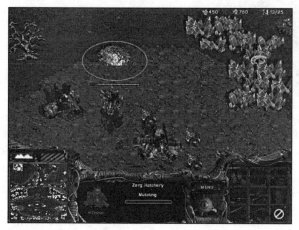

Fig. 2-27:

It takes the life of one Drone to create each structure you need.

ULTRALISK

Armor: Heavy

Hit Points: 400

Ground Attack: 20

Air Attack: 0

Attack Range: 1

Gas Required: 200

Minerals Required: 200

The Ultralisk may be a biological unit, but for general purposes you can consider it a powerful tank. With its 400 hit points, the Ultralisk is a powerhouse that can take down medium-sized enemy units easily. Although it's slow, it should be a part of every balance strike force.

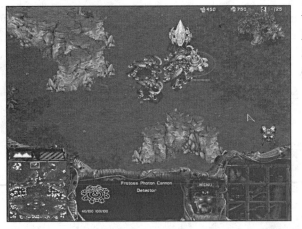

Fig. 2-28:

Four or five Ultralisks can level an enemy base in no time at all.

The Ultralisk's one limitation is that it's a big unit, and if many small units (such as Zerglings) attack it at once, it will take far more hits than it has as it destroys the enemy one at a time. For this reason it's often a good idea to keep some support units nearby to back up the Ultralisk if it gets into trouble. Protect your Ultralisks from these kinds of attacks and they can last you an entire scenario.

Fig. 2-29:

Lone Ultralisks can be shredded by Zerglings, so always keep support units handy.

Some players like to use their Ultralisks for mop-up after flushing the main enemy force from their base. Other units would do most of the fighting while the Ultralisks hang back and wait for the calm. After the situation is stabilized (that is, when all the enemy units are dead), the Ultralisks can come in and make short work of the enemy infrastructure.

DEFILER

Armor: Medium

Hit Points: 80

Ground Attack: 0

Air Attack: 0

Attack Range: 4

Gas Required: 100

Minerals Required: 25

The Defiler is a relatively high-level Zerg creature. It requires plenty of research to bring it up to attack standards. However, once it's up to snuff it can provide some very helpful abilities for your swarm.

As can many Zerg units, the Defiler can burrow. There are two main reasons to do so:

   ✳ to regain lost health or energy after an attack;

   ✳ to lie in wait for unsuspecting enemy units to wander by.

In either case, burrowing requires that you monitor your units frequently, keeping an eye out for an opportune time to pop back to the surface.

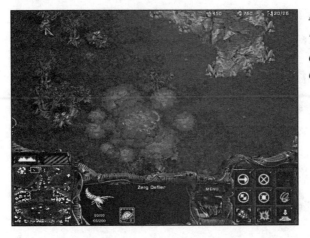

Fig. 2-30:

The Dark Swarm can provide excellent cover from airborne enemy units.

The Dark Swarm ability may not seem to have a lot of practical applications, but it does. Dark Swarm is basically a form of air cover for your units. Launching a Dark Swarm over a group of your ground units under attack can protect from airborne peril.

The Plague is somewhat like Terran Science vessels' Irradiate ability. It can cover a fairly large area with putrid gases and damaging spores. One effective way to use the Plague is to send a couple Zerglings toward an enemy base; when a bunch of enemies come out to fight, launch the Plague at them. It may not kill them, but biological creatures will sustain significant damage.

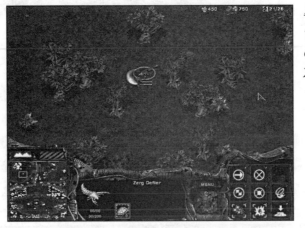

Fig. 2-31:

The Defiler can restore its energy by eating another of your Zerg creatures. Yuck.

Hungry? The Defilers' other ability is that of eating a fellow Zerg using the Consume command. This seems a little stomach-turning, but a Zergling is a small price to pay for a much-needed boost in energy for a Dark Swarm or a Plague. It might even be a good idea to group a couple of Zerglings with the Defilers so they'll have something to consume when their energy gets low.

INFESTED TERRAN

Armor: Light

Hit Points: 60

Ground Attack: 500

Air Attack: 0

Attack Range: 1

Gas Required: 50

Minerals Required: 100

You may not get many chances to use the Infested Terran in single-player *StarCraft*; however, it's an important unit. After you infest a Terran Command Center, you can produce these zombie-like kamikaze soldiers. When they get close to the enemy, they explode into a very powerful cloud of toxic gases, and the concussion devastates nearby units.

Fig. 2-32:

An Infested Terran is an impressive weapon, but it's hard to get.

To infest a Command Center, you must first damage it into the "red zone." Then you must hurry to get a Queen to infest it before it explodes (remember, Terran units pushed into the red zone deteriorate until they explode).

SPORE COLONY

Armor: Heavy

Hit Points: 400

Ground Attack: 0

Air Attack: 15*

Attack Range: 7

Gas Required: 0

Minerals Required: 50

Attack value limited against some units (see Appendix A).

The Spore Colony attacks passing air units and, as a detector unit, spots cloaked vessels or units of any kind. The Spore Colony is converted from a Creep Colony and continues to nourish the Creep.

Fig. 2-33:

Spore Colonies are best placed in groups of three or four for protection.

As with Missile Turrets (Terran) and Photon Cannons (Protoss), the Spore Colony is best used defensively in bunches. Several Spore Colonies can defend each other, making it less likely that a concentrated enemy attack will destroy any one colony.

SUNKEN COLONY

Armor: Heavy

Hit Points: 400

Ground Attack: 30

Air Attack: 0

Attack Range: 7

Gas Required: 0

Minerals Required: 75

The Sunken Colony is sister to the Spore Colony and defends against ground-based attacks. As does the Spore Colony, the Sunken Colony derives from the Creep Colony and continues to nourish the Creep even after conversion. Sunken Colonies work by thrusting a huge, tongue-like appendage under the ground toward their opponent. The tendril that emerges does plenty of damage to the enemy.

Fig. 2-34:

Like Spore Colonies, Sunken Colonies benefit from tight groupings.

Placing Sunken Colonies close together is even more effective than grouping Spore Colonies. Any units venturing onto the Creep where there are three or four Sunken Colonies will be pushing up daisies in seconds. Sunken Colonies are a crucial Zerg defense, so don't skimp.

EGG

Armor: Heavy
Hit Points: 200
Ground Attack: 0
Air Attack: 0
Attack Range: 0
Gas Required: 0
Minerals Required: 0

The Egg is simply a Larva mutating into a unit. Eggs are surprisingly resilient; it's unusual to see an Egg destroyed before it has a chance to hatch, although it can happen. If your Eggs are under attack, try to distract the attacker until the Egg can hatch.

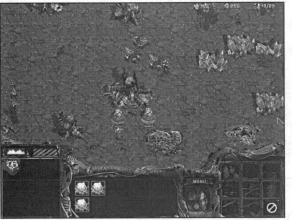

Fig. 2-35:

Eggs are surprisingly tough, but they can be killed if the enemy is persistent.

Air Units

The Zerg have a variety of air units, each geared to specific tasks. This can be a great advantage, but it can be difficult to anticipate which units you'll need in a given situation. Fortunately, Zerg air units cost the least of any race's, making it possible for you to have a balanced ground attack *and* a balanced air attack!

MUTALISK

Armor: Light

Hit Points: 120

Ground Attack: 9

Air Attack: 9

Attack Range: 3

Gas Required: 100

Minerals Required: 100

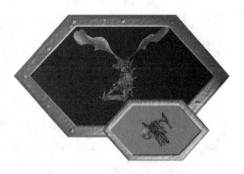

The Mutalisk is the Zerg basic air unit. It has nicely balanced air and ground attacks, and is relatively cheap. It's possible to play a complete mission using no other air units (besides Overlords, of course).

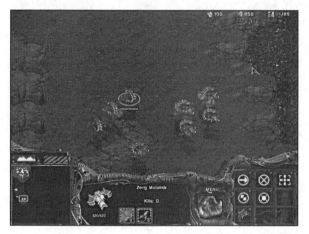

Fig. 2-36:

"Just say no" to your own death. Use Mutalisks in groups of three or more.

The Mutalisk's Glave Wurm attack, which keeps bouncing from enemy unit to enemy unit, can have excellent results if you use it properly. A Mutalisk's attack hits its target and then continues to another nearby unit or structure. This cumulative attack can be devastating when a large group of Mutalisks attacks a bunch of Marines. As the Mutalisks' shots rain down, each breaks away and hits another Marine, then breaks away again, and so on. The damage factor decreases by half every time the Wurm splits, but even so, the multiple attack values of multiple Mutalisks add up quickly.

Fig. 2-37:

The cumulative effects of the Mutalisk's multiple attacks can wreak havoc on a group of Marines.

The Mutalisk's major downside is its poor range (3), making it necessary for it to get very close to its target. This means Marines (with a range of 4) have an easy time against Mutalisks. As with all units, however, in force they're very effective in most situations.

GUARDIAN

Armor: Heavy

Hit Points: 150

Ground Attack: 20

Air Attack: 0

Attack Range: 8

Gas Required: 100

Minerals Required: 50

Guardians are actually Mutalisks that have metamorphosed after entering a cocooned state. You must earn the ability to create Guardians, and this usually won't happen until your base is fairly well-established. The Guardian is a bomber. Its sole purpose is to hurl explosive gobs of acid at ground targets. Its awesome attack power (20) packs enough of a wallop to take out a Missile Turret in 10 hits (or 1 hit each from a group of 10 Guardians).

Fig. 2-38:

The Guardian must metamorphose from a Mutalisk.

Guardians work best when used in groups of 10 or more. A single volley from such a group can destroy any enemy unit that has 200 or fewer hit points. Of course, 12 Guardians bombing an enemy base won't bomb it for long if the enemy attacks with air units: The Guardian is air-to-ground only. This is why it's important to have Mutalisks standing by to defend the Guardians.

Fig. 2-39:

In bunches the Guardians are bombers from hell, but they're very vulnerable to air attacks.

Expense is another limiting factor. Creating a Guardian not only costs 100 gas and 50 minerals, but you must metamorphose it from a Mutalisk, which has a price tag of 100 gas and 150 minerals. This means creating a Guardian costs 200 gas and 150 minerals altogether (ouch), so protecting that investment is very important.

QUEEN

Armor: Medium

Hit Points: 120

Ground Attack: 0

Air Attack: 0

Attack Range: 0

Gas Required: 150

Minerals Required: 100

The Queen is a unique unit. Although it lacks the ability to attack enemy units directly, it can use its special abilities to great effect. Because the Queen isn't particularly expensive, you can create a small pack for backup, defense, fire-fighting, or to use as first-strike units.

The first, and maybe the handiest, of the Queen's special abilities is the Parasite. This tiny organism infects an enemy unit and allows you (the player) to see through its eyes. It can be prudent to take a Queen and move about the map (carefully) depositing Parasites on any unit it encounters. Airborne units, such as Dropships or patrolling Scouts, are ideal to infect with a Parasite because they constantly move around the map, giving you an excellent view of what's going on behind enemy lines.

Fig. 2-40:

Ensnare's green goo tells you the ability is working.

The Ensnare ability can aid your forces greatly. When you launch Ensnare, enemy units become engulfed in a green goo that slows them down, making it easier for your units to take them out. You can use Ensnare offensively to bog down enemy units while your attackers file by.

Spawning Broodlings is a spectacular way to use your Queens. Spawn Broodlings shoot spores into the enemy; those spores then hatch into Broodlings that feed on the host. This all happens very quickly, and in the end the host explodes, leaving behind a pair of Broodlings ready to do your bidding.

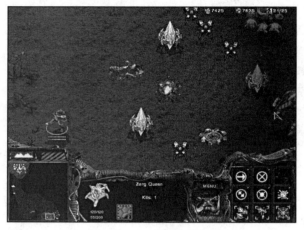

Fig. 2-41:

Spawn Broodlings quickly get some vicious little critters behind enemy lines.

Use Infestation to capture a badly damaged Terran Command Center and get Infested Terrans. To infest a Command Center you need to get a Queen close enough to one that's in the red zone (nearly destroyed) and launch Infestation at it. The Command Center then will fall under Zerg control, alowing you to create Infested Terrans.

SCOURGE

Armor: Light

Hit Points: 20

Ground Attack: 0

Air Attack: 110

Attack Range: 1

Gas Required: 75

Minerals Required: 25

The Scourge are the Zerglings of the air. They hatch two at a time from each Egg and cost only slightly more than Zerglings, making it relatively easy to create large groups of them. It's a good idea to keep a group of 12 Scourge around for emergencies in case a capital ship attacks.

Fig. 2-42:

The Scourge are famous for being Carrier killers.

The Scourge is essentially a kamikaze, slamming into the hull of a larger ship and exploding on contact. They really shine against Terran Carriers; in fact, many *Star-Craft* players call them "Carrier killers." A group of 12 Scourge flung at a Carrier will almost certainly destroy it, making the Scourge a valuable commodity. The downside is they fight less well against smaller ships, and can't attack ground units.

OVERLORD

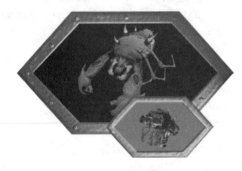

Armor: Heavy

Hit Points: 200

Ground Attack: 0

Air Attack: 0

Attack Range: 0

Gas Required: 0

Minerals Required: 100

The Overlord serves three purposes for the Zerg: First, it's the equivalent of Terran Supply Depots or Protoss Pylons, and how many you need depends on how large the Zerg force is. Second, the Overlord is the Zerg Shuttle. To transport units by air, you must research Transport for your Overlords (which can be done in a Lair). The Overlord is also a detection unit, which allows sighting of cloaked units!

Obviously, transporting units with an Overlord is risky. However, if you take the proper precautions, it needn't be stress-inducing. First, protect your Overlords with Mutalisks and Scourge. Second, don't move your Overlords into areas that have lots of anti-air resistance. Third, upgrade your Overlord Sight and Speed in the Lair/Hive. Speed is especially important, because the upgrade doubles the lumbering Overlord's rate of movement.

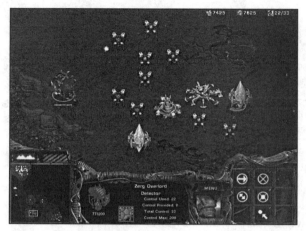

Fig. 2-43:

Overlords are easy targets for Photon Cannons and Missile Turrets, so don't take them into hostile territory unless you have a very good reason.

Zerg Structures

The most important thing to remember about Zerg structures is that they're living organisms and can heal themselves after taking a beating. This makes a substantial difference in how you manage your resources. For example, a structure that's near death might normally be replaced, but in the case of the Zerg, the structure will slowly regain its hit points over time.

This principle makes protecting damaged structures more important than it is with other races and changes the scenario's complexion in terms of both Zerg and enemy strategy. The enemy might launch a last-ditch second effort to finish off a badly damaged building rather than see its failed attack go to waste as the structure repairs itself. For the Zerg, an offensive push might be in order after fending off an attack, if only to clear the enemy out of your base so the structures have time to heal. Of course, this depends largely on your opponent's playing style, but the principles hold true.

SUNKEN AND SPORE COLONIES

Sunken Colonies and Spore Colonies both derive from the Creep Colony and both continue to feed the Creep even after conversion. These two units will be largely responsible for defending your main Creep, and so you should build them in quantity whenever possible, positioning Spore Colonies throughout the base as an air deterrent, and distributing Sunken Colonies only where ground-based attacks are possible.

THE PROTOSS FORCE

As you might expect, the Protoss differ in several ways from both the Terrans and the Zerg. They're the most technologically advanced race, but also pay the greatest base cost per unit. By the time you're playing as the Protoss, you'll have finished all the Zerg and Terran missions and should have a solid grip on *StarCraft* strategy. Nevertheless, there are a few things you should know before you venture forth.

Protoss units enter each scenario through a Probe-opened Warp Rift. The cool thing about Probes is they need only begin the process of opening the rift; they don't have to wait for the structure to appear. This way you can have a single Probe move around opening Warp Rifts while your other Probes happily harvest minerals and gas.

Playing as the Zerg may leave you with a throwaway attitude toward your units. Protoss units are considerably more expensive than the Zerg's, however, so never treat them as if they're easy to replace. Novice Protoss players have lost many a game by running out of resources trying to create overwhelming numbers. The key to Protoss victory lies in using superior technology rather than brute force.

Another Protoss feature worth mentioning: They all have shields that absorb punishment before a unit takes any hits. Actual damage can't be repaired, but the shields always regenerate. This means a Protoss unit can have one hit point left and, if its shields have regenerated, it can still be a threat. A Terran EMP blast can defeat your shields in one fell swoop, but otherwise they must be taken out one hit at a time.

Ground Units

Get ready to explore *StarCraft*'s "high-tech" lineup of ground units. "Strong," "powerful," "fast," and "expensive" all describe the Protoss ground arsenal, but in the end it's a well-balanced set of units that stacks up fairly evenly against the other races' units.

ZEALOT

Armor: Light

Shield: 80

Hit Points: 80

Ground Attack: 16

Air Attack: 0

Attack Range: 1

Gas Required: 0

Minerals Required: 100

Like the Marine and the Zergling for the Terrans and the Zergs, the Zealot is the Protoss ground force's base unit. The Zealot, however, is in a different league from its opposing counterparts when it comes to attack ability. The Zealot has almost three times the attack power of the Marine and literally four times the Zergling's. However, nothing in life is free, and the Zealot is the most expensive base unit by 100 percent. You pay for what you get.

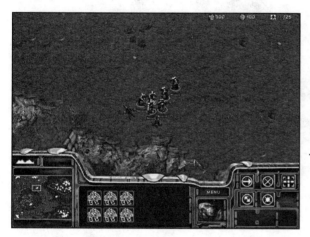

Fig. 2-44:

The Zealot is the basic ground unit of your dreams: It packs an attack of 16 and is tough enough to stand up to almost any ground attack. The downside? Zealots get pummeled from the skies.

The Zealot's weapon is the Psionic Blade. He has two (one on each arm). Thus, the Zealot has no ranged attack and must be very close to the enemy to do damage—and he can't attack air units. For this reason, it's always a good idea to take along Dragoons, Scouts, or the Templars (with Psionic Storm) to defend against air attacks whenever your Zealots are on the move. A large group of Zealots can destroy an enemy base quickly if nothing attacks from the sky.

DRAGOON

Armor: Heavy

Shield: 80

Hit Points: 100

Ground Attack: 20*

Air Attack: 20*

Attack Range: 4

Gas Required: 50

Minerals Required: 150

* Attack value limited against some units (see Appendix A).

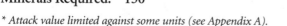

The Dragoon is the number two unit of the Protoss force. It's a powerful unit, but it has a longer cool-down time between firing, and is considerably more expensive and time-consuming to produce than the Zealot. However, the Dragoon is proficient at performing both ground and air attacks and can attack on its own volition or back up fellow units.

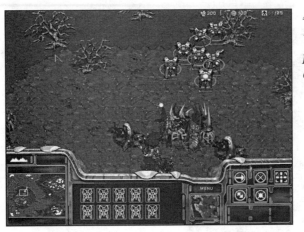

Fig. 2-45:

The Dragoon is excellent for performing both ground and air attacks.

Because Dragoons are fast, you may be tempted to make a strike force of 10 or so to take it to the enemy—but don't. The Dragoon is an excellent unit, but 30 Zerglings will be more than 12 Dragoons can handle if there are no backup units. A popular tactic is to move groups of Zealots and Dragoons together in much the same way Marines and Firebats are used together.

Fig. 2-46:

Taking eight high-priced Dragoons into a pile of 30 Zerglings will give you a lesson in humility.

It's also a good idea to keep a small group of Dragoons around your base to add firepower to your Photon Cannon defenses. Keeping units at home is always a good idea, but Dragoons are so fast you can move them to a hot spot without losing much time. They're a very effective mobile unit when you need a little help quickly.

REAVER

Armor: Heavy

Shield: 80

Hit Points: 100

Ground Attack (Scarab Drone):   100*

Air Attack: 0

Attack Range: 8

Gas Required: 100

Minerals Required: 200

* Attack value limited against some units (see Appendix A).

The Reaver is a strange unit. It's often called the "Ground Carrier" because of the Scarab Drones it unleashes on the enemy. Although it looks intimidating, it doesn't have any weapons of its own. Instead, it builds Scarab Drones in its internal manufacturing plant and unleashes *them* on the enemy.

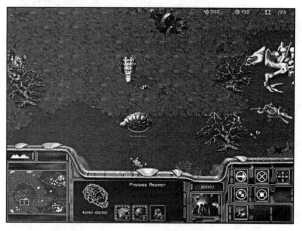

Fig. 2-47:

The Reaver is slow, expensive, and doesn't have a main weapon, but it still rocks.

The Reaver can store as many as 10 Scarabs within itself and use them as necessary. When released, the Scarabs zip toward their targets and explode, causing substantial damage to friendly and enemy units alike. Don't send Scarabs into packs of fighting units unless you're prepared to take some friendly fire.

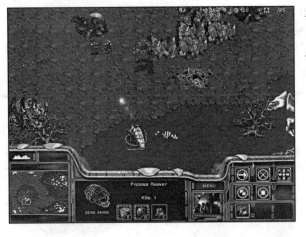

Fig. 2-48:

Use care when deploying your Scarabs or you'll end up taking out your own forces.

Reavers are very effective against defensive emplacements such as Bunkers or Spore Colonies. However, the Reaver is fairly easy to kill, so protect it as much as possible; if it looks like you may lose a Reaver, use up the Scarabs it has left!

HIGH TEMPLAR

Armor: Light

Shield: 40

Hit Points: 40

Ground Attack: 0

Air Attack: 0

Attack Range: 3

Gas Required: 150

Minerals Required: 50

Although High Templars can fight, you should keep them back from the front lines and use their psychic abilities to your advantage. These units are veterans of Protoss armies who mastered the Psi energy that runs through their bodies.

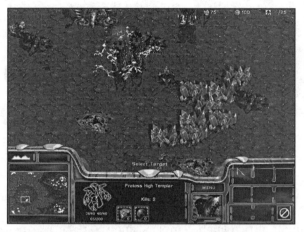

Fig. 2-49:

The High Templars aren't designed for hand-to-hand combat. Stick to their Psionic abilities and you'll be OK.

The Psionic Storm is their most powerful psionic ability. It can take out groups of enemy units if they're grouped close together and don't have much room to run. Because the Zerg tend to move and attack en masse, the Psionic Storm can kill off large numbers of them. Try sending a single Zealot onto a Zerg Creep. When the Hydralisks and Zerglings pop out to fight, hit them with a Psionic Storm and watch them turn to pools of blood.

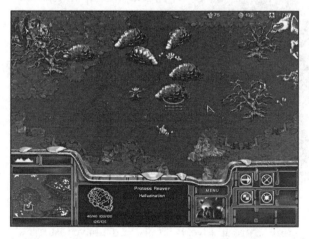

Fig. 2-50:

The Hallucination can fool the enemy into thinking you have more units than you really do.

Hallucination is valuable when your forces are outnumbered. It produces two copies of each unit you use it on. You can see which units are real and which aren't, but the enemy can't and often will attack the hallucinations.

The Summon Archon ability effectively joins two High Templars to create one super-unit. The two Templars are forever merged into an Archon, a powerful unit that is devestating against both ground and air units.

ARCHON

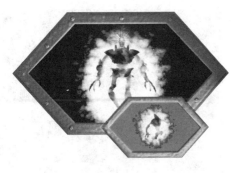

Armor: Heavy
Shield: 350
Hit Points: 10
Ground Attack: 30
Air Attack: 30
Attack Range: 3
Gas Required: 300
Minerals Required: 100

Archons are created from the union of two High Templars, and so are fairly expensive. However, their attacks and defensive shields are so powerful they're usually worth the expense. The Archon is also special because it can attack units both in the air and on the ground. Indeed, a group of seven or eight Archons is tough for any race to stop, especially if they have backup.

Fig. 2-51:

With 350 shield points, the Archon is a devastating unit.

Use the Archon as what it really is—a Heavy Assault Warrior. Building up a devastating Archon strike force can be counterproductive. If it fails, you'll have lost massive amounts of resources. Instead, use Archons to complement groupings of Dragoons and Zealots. Your Archon can dish out massive amounts of pain on any powerful enemy before it can kill your more vulnerable units.

PHOTON CANNON

Armor: Heavy

Shield: 100

Hit Points: 100

Ground Attack: 20*

Air Attack: 20*

Attack Range: 7

Gas Required: 0

Minerals Required: 150

* Attack value limited against some units (see Appendix A).

The Photon Cannon is perhaps the game's best defensive structure. Its cost is reasonable and it can defend against land and air targets as far as seven clicks distant. A webbing of four to six Photon Cannons near a contentious point can spell the difference between victory and defeat.

Fig. 2-52:

A grid of Photon Cannons can be all the defense you'll ever need.

The Photon Cannon's downside is that it's relatively easy to destroy—so once you've set up a Defensive Matrix, keep a Probe handy in case you need to open a Warp Rift and bring in replacements.

PROBE

> Armor: Light
>
> Shield: 20
>
> Hit Points: 20
>
> Ground Attack: 5
>
> Air Attack: 0
>
> Attack Range: 1
>
> Gas Required: 0
>
> Minerals Required: 50

At 20 hit points, the Protoss Probe has the lowest HP total of any enemy counterpart, but its ability to open Warp Rifts and walk away makes up for this. Like the Terran SCV and Zerg Drone, the Probe can fight the enemy, but with so little defense (and with such a feeble attack) it's wiser to rely on Photon Cannons around your base.

Fig. 2-53:

The Probe is a great base-building unit, so avoid using it for fighting.

When setting up a base, use all your Probes but one to gather resources. It can open all the Warp Rifts you need without interrupting the flow of resources.

Air Units

As with the other Protoss units, Protoss air units tend to be expensive, but again, they're also very powerful. If you can amass a large enough resource base, you can build the air units you need to win. Many players believe *StarCraft* is won and lost in the skies. That's open to interpretation, but never doubt the importance of having a solid "air force."

SCOUT

Armor: Heavy

Shield: 90

Hit Points: 130

Ground Attack: 8

Air Attack: 24*

Attack Range: 4

Gas Required: 100

Minerals Required: 300

* Attack value limited against some units (see Appendix A).

Building "victory fleets" of Scouts to fly around kicking butt is a popular pastime, but it's probably not the wisest course to take. Creating such a group requires crushing amounts of mineral resources. The Scout may sound like it's—well, a scout, but it's really more like a full-featured fighter than a reconnaissance ship. The Scout can attack both air and ground targets, although it's best suited for air-to-air combat.

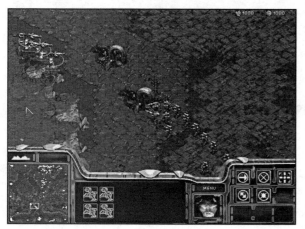

Fig. 2-54:

Use the Scout in small groups to flank enemy forces.

Scouts are an excellent way to flank the enemy, ideally in groups of three to five. If you attack an enemy force from the front, bring two groups of three Scouts each against enemy flanks to cause a chaotic enemy overcorrection that can yield you the battle.

**Fig. 2-55:**

A Scout or two around your base is worth three in the bush.

Their great speed makes Scouts the perfect Protoss firefighters, flying from hot spot to hot spot to keep the peace when the enemy gets too cocky. Of course, this includes attacks on your own base, so keep at least one Scout at home to be on the safe side.

CARRIER

Armor: Heavy

Shield: 150

Hit Points: 250

Ground Attack (Interceptors):   5

Air Attack (Interceptors):   5

Attack Range: 8

Gas Required: 300

Minerals Required: 350

The Carrier is perhaps _StarCraft_'s most powerful weapon. The Carrier itself has no innate attack ability. However, after you upgrade it, it can hold up to eight Interceptors that can each attack air and ground units with a value of 5. In other words, a pair of Carriers can unleash a hornet's nest of Interceptors that can destroy air and ground units alike in a frenzied bloodbath.

Fig. 2-56:

A fully loaded Carrier is an awesome weapon that can send the enemy into a state of panic.

The Carrier can land the killing blow on an enemy your forces are attacking. Even if the battle is a standoff, a fully loaded Carrier or two can turn the tide of the battle in a hurry. By bringing a Carrier into an area of enemy units, and clicking to "attack" a general location, your Interceptors will hunt continually for new targets. They'll swarm and swarm until there's nothing left to kill. Interceptors often will draw the attention (and fire) of enemy units and structures, but they're so fast they rarely take a hit.

Fig. 2-57:

A few Battlecruisers can take out a Carrier in one shot, so don't get cocky.

As good as they sound, Carriers aren't invulnerable. A group of 12 Scourge ("Carrier Killers") can bring an end to a Carrier in about 10 seconds. And a trio of Battlecruisers with the Yamato Gun can take out a Carrier in one shot. This doesn't mean you shouldn't use Carriers; just don't rely on them too heavily.

ARBITER

Armor: Heavy

Shield: 150

Hit Points: 200

Ground Attack: 10*

Air Attack: 10*

Attack Range: 5

Gas Required: 500

Minerals Required: 25

* Attack value limited against some units (see Appendix A).

The Arbiter is an interesting ship that provides three key functions for the Protoss. While it's a somewhat capable warship that can attack units on the ground or in the air, its innate abilities make this vessel an essential part of a balanced Protoss fleet.

The Arbiter emanates a Cloak around the ship, concealing any units within that radius. The Arbiter itself isn't cloaked, but it looks a heck of a lot less threatening approaching an enemy base than a fleet of four Carriers. Only detector units can see them coming.

Fig. 2-58:

Arbiters can hide more ships than you might think, but its Cloak is useless around detector units.

Recall is another powerful Arbiter ability. It acts like a teleport for units within a certain radius. A few Arbiters near the front lines can teleport groups of units to the action instantaneously using its Recall ability, bypassing the time-consuming and risky business of using Shuttles. There are plenty of other ways to use Recall, including teleporting units to an undefended base that's come under attack.

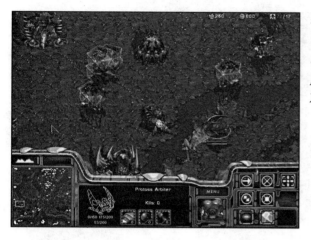

Fig. 2-59:

Use the Stasis Field to disable enemy units and even the playing field (or tilt it toward you).

The Stasis Field is a powerful ability that can reduce the burden of combat substantially. For example, if your forces come up against a large enemy group, you can put half of the enemy group in a Stasis Field while you attack (and kill) the other half. When the Stasis Field wears off, you can kill *those* units. Basically, you can use the Stasis Field to take several enemy units out of the picture until you're ready to deal with them.

OBSERVER

Armor: Light

Shield: 20

Hit Points: 40

Ground Attack: 0

Air Attack: 0

Attack Range: 0

Gas Required: 75

Minerals Required: 25

An Observer is a permanently cloaked scout unit that's also a detector (it can see other cloaked units). It's usually a good idea to place a few Observers over strategic points on the map (such as resource nodes) to monitor enemy troop movement. Because they're cloaked, they can be your best source of enemy intelligence, so keep one or two in action at all times.

Fig. 2-60:

"Keeping up with the Joneses" is an important part of StarCraft, and a pair of Observers can help you see what the Joneses are up to.

SHUTTLE

Armor: Heavy

Shield: 60

Hit Points: 80

Ground Attack: 0

Air Attack: 0

Attack Range: 0

Gas Required: 0

Minerals Required: 200

The Shuttle is, well, the Shuttle. In the case of the Protoss, it's the only mechanical way to move units through the air. The Arbiter can use its Recall ability to move units faster, but the Shuttle is still an effective way to ferry troops across large or impassable areas.

Fig. 2-61:

Shuttles are important units even for the high-flying Protoss.

Protoss Structures

Protoss structures have no special ability to heal (like the Zerg) or move (like the Terran), but they do have shields that recharge continually. This defensive boost provides the protection necessary to survive attacks from competitors. The fact that Probes needn't sit around waiting for structures to be built helps you acquire more structures sooner than would be possible otherwise. One Probe can do the work of opening the Warp Rifts, while all the others collect resources.

PHOTON CANNONS

The Photon Cannon is the all-purpose Protoss defensive weapon structure, and it serves that function well. Able to attack both air and ground targets, a grouping of Photon Cannons can provide enough of a deterrent to permanently halt attacks from human opponents, and if the computer is bent on continuing, the "Photon grid" will mow the enemy down. Always keep at least three closely placed Photon Cannons at your base entrance(s).

Chapter 3:

GENERAL
STRATEGY

In addition to having an excellent story line, incredible cutscenes, and great action, StarCraft is a fascinating strategy game. For this reason more than any other, it's critically important to use strategies proven to help achieve victory. Feel free to experiment, but realize that failing to follow at least a basic strategic framework can lead to bitter defeat.

The following general strategies for all three races have the blessing of the Blizzard testing department, so it's probably a good idea to familiarize yourself with them.

Players often want to know things such as, "Which race is the most powerful?" The answer is simple, but it's probably not what you want to hear. StarCraft is a very well-balanced game, and it's possible to win no matter which race you use. Each has its strengths and weaknesses, and each can inspire unique strategies. Although you'll find ideas for strategies throughout this book, by all means push the strategic envelope and seek the new wrinkles that can give you an edge.

Special thanks must go out to Blizzard employees Rob Pardo, Eric Dodds, Frank Gilson, and Derek Simmons for their infinite strategic wisdom.

 The strategies and tips given in this chapter can apply to both the single and multiplayer games.

THE TERRANS

The Terrans are the "middle-of-the-road" race that has a balance of numbers (of units) and technology. Because you cut your teeth on them, they're your first ambassadors to the world of StarCraft. There are probably as many Terran attack and defense strategies as there are players, but these key ideas will help you through the rough stuff.

General Strategies and Tips

* Hotkey the Comsat Station (yes, you can do that) to 9 and 0. This way you can get a Sensor Sweep quickly without having to click on your Comsat Station. You can get a sweep on demand by pressing the station key and then **S**. Getting a Sensor Sweep can be critical if your troops are under attack from cloaked units, because the sweep will reveal enemy unit locations.

* For defense, build Bunkers (filled with Marines) and Missile Turrets together and place Siege Tanks beside them. This combination provides an extremely tenacious defense that's very difficult for the enemy to penetrate.

* When both Comsat Stations and Yamato Guns become available, use them together to take advantage of the Yamato's superior range. For example, when you want to take out a Missile Turret, sweep the Missile Turret area with a Sensor Sweep and then target it with a Yamato strike. The Battlecruiser will move in to take its shot but it will still be outside the Missile Turret's range.

* This is a little underhanded, but it can be very effective: Build a Factory or Barracks behind the enemy's position and start cranking out units for a backside attack. If you can't afford to build there, or can't get an SCV to that position, fly an existing structure into position and then begin building.

* Use the Science Vessel's Irradiate ability on biological units. This can be very effective, even against Templars or Defilers.

* Use Bunkers to prevent enemy movement. Place them at any choke point the enemy must squeeze through to advance. Before it's destroyed, a carefully placed Bunker can do huge amounts of damage to the advancing enemy.

* Use Bunkers in a "leapfrog" tactic (as Frank Gilson puts it), building them one after another, ever deeper into enemy territory, with the previous Bunker protecting the Bunker under construction. This method is particularly useful against the Zerg.

Against the Zerg

✳ Build lots of Firebats. The Zerg are an organic race with mostly ground-based attacks. Firebats are always a cost-effective unit to use against Zerg ground minions.

✳ Use Battlecruisers more for defense than offense, especially in multiplayer games. This is because the Zerg Scourges can take out a Battlecruiser for half the cost. In a resource battle, you'd lose.

✳ If a unit becomes infected with a Parasite, the enemy can see everything *it* sees, so use the infected unit to fight the enemy. Never keep it around your base.

✳ Take out enemy Guardians at all costs. A group of Guardians can reduce your base to rubble very quickly. Keep Wraiths or Battlecruisers around for this purpose.

✳ Whatever you do, don't leave an outpost Command Center for the Zerg to infest. If this happens, you'll quickly have Infested Terrans blowing up around you, and that isn't pretty.

✳ When attacking a Zerg base, always take out the underlying tech-tree buildings first. You may be tempted to go for the Hatcheries, but you can cripple your opponent more by taking out the structures necessary for building advanced units. Take Zerg structures out in this (or any) order: Spire, Ultralisk Cavern, Hydralisk Den, Spawning Pool, and Queen's Nest.

Against the Protoss

* Again, Firebats are important, but only against Zealots, so don't go crazy building them. Make just enough to keep Zealot groups at bay.

* Build Ghosts for defense. They're a little too expensive to produce in bulk for offense. However, when an enemy Carrier or Reaver comes by, you can use the Lockdown ability to neutralize them.

* Use Science Vessels. Their EMP ability is especially effective against the Protoss (it removes their shields). The EMP is as effective for attack as it is for defense.

* If the Protoss are employing Arbiters, use a Yamato Gun to take them out quickly and reveal cloaked units.

* Watch out for Observers. They cloak and will locate your own cloaked units. Use a Comsat Sensor Sweep to check for Observers in areas where you plan to use cloaked units.

* Keep Missile Turrets around your entire base as an early warning system. If this technique prevents just one Shuttle from dropping a pair of Reavers, it's worth it.

THE ZERG

Because the Zerg are entirely biological and don't have all the high-end units of the Protoss or Terrans, they must employ different tactics to achieve the same ends.

General Strategies and Tips

* When enemy air units enter your base, have a Defiler use a Dark Swarm over your Hydralisks. This renders them impervious to enemy air attacks and frees them to shoot the bad guys out of the sky.

* Build Zerglings and Hydralisks, initially, but remember that Zealots and Firebats can go through Zerglings like a hot knife through butter. Use your Zerglings and Hydralisks to attack Marines and Dragoons.

* Guardians are your heavy attack force. A group of 12 will destroy nearly any land-based group as long as they stay at a safe distance and are willing to retreat.

* On larger maps, use Nydus Canals to connect your bases. This allows you to build a much smaller defense force at each base, because you can teleport units from one base to another very quickly.

* The Scourge are most effective against enemy capital ships such as Carriers and Battlecruisers, so keep a bunch around for this. Note also that the Scourge are significantly less effective against Scouts or Wraiths, so don't waste them against these units.

* Try to keep a large perimeter of Sunken Colonies and Spore Colonies around important structures in your base. This way, even if you leave your base lightly defended, the colonies can work to eliminate the enemy threat.

* When attacking an enemy base with a strictly Zergling force, don't waste time attacking enemy units. Instead, send your Zerglings to attack enemy structures; a group of Zerglings can bring down a structure quickly.

* The Zerg ability to create masses of a certain type of unit by morphing multiple Larvae can quickly shift the tide of battle in your favor, if you choose the units well. Keeping extra Hatcheries around is an excellent way to increase your ability to manufacture plenty of new units quickly.

Against the Terrans

* Use Queens to defend against Wraiths. Have your Queen use its Ensnare ability on a group of cloaked Wraiths, and then put Parasites on as many of them as you can (this removes their ability to cloak).

* To take out a Terran player quickly, build lots of Zerglings. Upgrade their speed and attack abilities, and then launch them at the enemy in groups of 12. Speed is important; you don't want the Terrans to build up a large force of Firebats.

* Always use Hydralisks, the Zergs' bread-and-butter unit. It can be effective in both ground and air attack and defense. A Zerg player without Hydralisks is a Zerg player who's probably losing.

* Use your Queen's Spawn Broodling ability on Tanks and Goliaths, and use Ensnare on cloaked Wraiths and Ghosts. If a cloaked unit is escaping, infest it with a Parasite so it can't cloak ever again.

* Use the Plague where Supply Depots are grouped closely together. After a few Plagues the affected depots will proceed into the red and eventually will blow up (unless repaired).

* Take advantage of your ability to infest a Terran Command Center. Try to attack one early on to open the door for Infestation. Remember, though, that you'll need a Queen for this, so don't risk any units until you're ready.

* Keep your Hydralisks and Zerglings burrowed until heavy enemy units come close; then spring the surprise. Keeping several groups of units burrowed in defensive positions is always a good idea.

Against the Protoss

✳ In the early going, build Hydralisks and more Hydralisks. They're very effective against Zealots, Dragoons, and Scouts.

✳ Watch out for Observers. Fortunately for the Zerg, the Overlord is a detector unit, and you usually have plenty of Overlords to patrol key areas around your base and resource centers.

✳ When attacking a Protoss base, always attack the Pylons near Gateways and Stargates first. Once you take the Pylons out, the buildings lose their power and become useless to Protoss forces. Beware, however, of Probes that probably will scoot out to warp in new Pylons.

✳ Build up plenty of defensive structures around your base(s). Zealots can make dog meat out of a lone Sunken Colony quickly, so always cross-protect your Colonies with at least two other units.

✳ Against Carriers, nothing can beat the Scourge's attack. A group of 12 Scourge can take out a Carrier in a few seconds, so always keep a group of inexpensive Scourge lying in wait.

✳ If any Arbiters come your way, have your Queens use Ensnare on units that might be hiding underneath the Arbiter's cloak.

THE PROTOSS

The Protoss are the most highly evolved race technologically. As such, they require special consideration when facing off against the other races. Because of the high cost of all Protoss units, you can't expect to win a war of attrition. Instead, you must use the powerful Protoss units you have to do the maximum damage possible.

General Strategies and Tips

✳ For the Protoss, base layout is key. Place your Pylons so they power your buildings but don't clutter your base, and put important tech-tree structures close together in a very protected area.

✳ Protoss Probes don't have to wait around to "build" a structure. They can simply open the Warp Rift and move on. This allows you to use all but one of your Probes for harvesting resources.

✳ Gas it up! More than any other race, the Protoss rely on Vespene Gas to build their high-priced units. Move to secure multiple Vespene Geysers whenever possible or you may end up sucking fumes.

✳ Although Photon Cannons are an excellent defensive unit, they're fairly expensive. Build them in groups so they can support one another; then make sure to build more than one Pylon to service them. As a rule of thumb, build two Pylons for every three Photon Cannons and you'll be OK.

✳ Have an Arbiter follow a unit in the group it's covering with its cloak. This way the Arbiter, although never actively engaged in battle, will follow just behind the attack force.

✳ Use the Templars' Hallucination ability. When attacking any large force, keep a good mix of hallucinated units in your front line. Done properly this can give you a huge advantage, because the enemy will waste many of their defensive attacks on units that don't exist.

✳ Throw a Templar or two in a Shuttle and move them to an area just behind an enemy mineral field. Then have your Templars use the Psionic Storm on the streams of enemy workers that approach to collect resources. It's underhanded, but it works.

✳ Put an Observer over each unowned mineral field. When the enemy comes to set up a base you'll know, and you can take it out before it can get established.

✳ Fly an Arbiter behind enemy lines and have it use its Recall ability to bring a group of Archons in. Sit back and survey the carnage.

✳ If you use Carriers, make sure you upgrade their capacity before you take them into battle. The difference between a non-upgraded Carrier and an upgraded one is considerable, so it's worth waiting until you've completed that technological advance.

Against the Terrans

* Large groups of Carriers are very powerful, but it's important to keep an Observer with your Carrier groups so you can spot cloaked Wraiths.

* In multiplayer games, be ready for the Firebat rush. A combination of Zealots, Dragoons, and Photon Cannons are your best defense early. Zealots alone generally are insufficient.

* Against Goliaths, Zealots are your best unit, but make sure they have their Speed upgrade before you try to chase one down. As with nearly all units, it's important to attack in force if you're pitting Zealots against Goliaths.

* Beware of pesky Science Vessels. An EMP used properly against your forces can rob you of your shields (until they regenerate). For this reason it's a good idea to keep your units a little spread out.

* Against Battlecruisers, use a combination of Carriers and Scouts. Try to outnumber the Battlecruisers. Ideally, you'll get a couple Arbiters to cloak your units while you attack.

* Keep a couple of Observers patrolling the base perimeter to check for cloaked Wraiths or Ghosts preparing to use Nukes.

Against the Zerg

* Don't allow Zerg Overlords to hang over your base. Build Dragoons to chase them away. Photon Cannons aren't always effective for this, because the Overlords will simply fly out of range. Never let the enemy know anything he or she doesn't have to know.

* Zerglings can destroy Photon Cannons very quickly, so make sure you have other troops handy to support your cannons in the face of an all-out rush.

* Try to keep an eye on all the units in your base. If a unit has caught a Parasite, use it against the enemy. For example, if a Zealot has been infested with a parasite, send it (along with a few other units) on an attack run against an auxiliary Zerg target (such as a small outpost) while you send a "real" attack force to the main Hive. Often the Zerg will pull their defenses toward the outpost, leaving the real target poorly defended.

* Mutalisks can be very effective against the Protoss, so build plenty of Dragoons and Scouts to defend against them. If a large group of Mutalisks attacks, counterattack in greater force, or you may lose your troops.

* Reavers are fantastic for attacking Zerg bases. Their Scarabs can decimate Zerg structures quickly, because Zerg bases usually are smaller and more efficient.

* If the enemy is using a lot of Zerglings against you, counter with Zealots. The Zerglings' small size makes them difficult to target, so use "Attack-Move" commands to get the Zealots into mop-up mode.

* The Scourge make Carriers a bad investment against the Zerg. A Carrier can cost up to 950 in resources and be destroyed by as few as five or six Scourge. That's a tough trade to swallow.

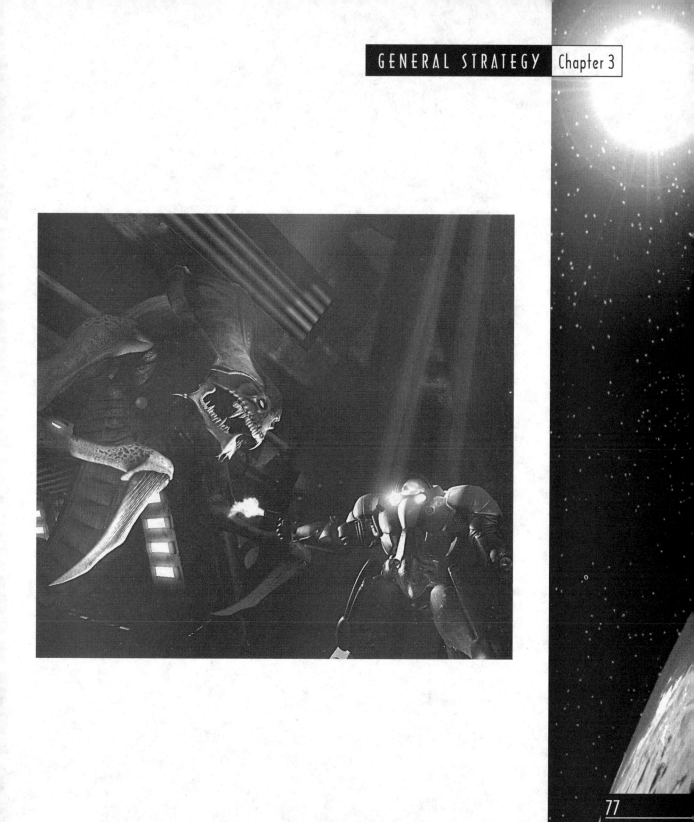

Chapter 4:

The
Terran
Missions

MISSION #1:

WASTELAND

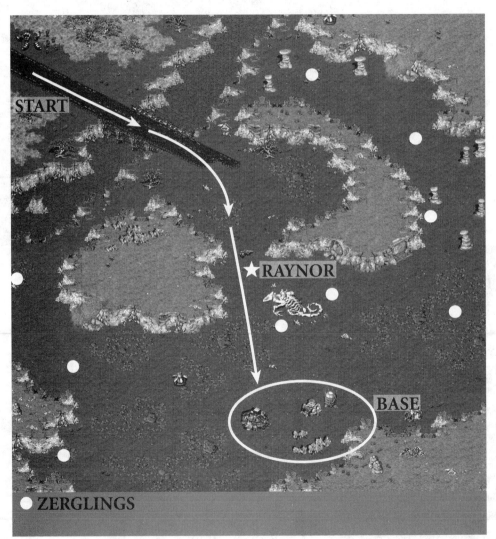

START

★ RAYNOR

BASE

● ZERGLINGS

Fig. 4-1:

Map of Terran Mission 1.

Mission Overview

The Confederate Security Forces have quarantined the entire planet of Mar Sara and will have implemented a complete lockdown within 48 hours. You must relocate your colonists—SCVs and Marines—to the wastelands. En route you'll meet up with Jim Raynor, the local marshal, who'll help you take out any enemies you may encounter.

Mission Objectives

* Find Jim Raynor.
* Build a Barracks.
* Train 10 Marines.
* Jim Raynor must survive.

Special Units

* Jim Raynor (in Vulture)

New Units

* Marines

Enemy Units

* Zerglings (Fenris Brood: dispersed throughout map)

Battle Strategy

Your Marines and SCVs start in the upper-left corner. The Command Center and Supply Depot lie some distance away in the lower-central map area. Divide your troops into two groups, Marines and SCVs, and move the Marines toward the Command Center. After passing the bridge you'll run into Jim Raynor and one or two isolated Zergling groups. Terminate the Zerglings with extreme prejudice. Then move down to provide support for the base. Once the base is secure, move your SCVs down and start mining minerals in earnest.

After retrieving sufficient minerals, build a Barracks and manufacture the 10 Marines you need to complete this mission. Jim Raynor and a couple of Marines can continue moving around the map mopping up Zerglings, but it's not necessary for victory. Remember, if you lose any Marines, you must replace them to hit the production target (10). Also, there's a slight chance you'll lose Jim Raynor in fighting the remaining Zerglings, so you may want just to sit tight and guard the Command Center area.

Fig. 4-2:

Divide your units into SCVs and Marines before you move south.

Fig. 4-3:

A few packs of Zerglings wait at different points around this map.

Resource Management

When your SCVs reach the Command Center, place them all on mineral-gathering duty until you've banked 150 minerals. Then get one of the SCVs to build a Barracks while the others continue retrieving minerals. During this time, use your Marines to guard the Command Center area: A few Zerglings may be waiting at various points around the periphery. Once the Barracks is in place, set it to build one Marine after another until you reach 10, when the mission will end. To see how many Marines you currently have and how many more you need, check out the Marine counter in the upper-left corner of the screen.

MISSION #2:
BACKWATER STATION

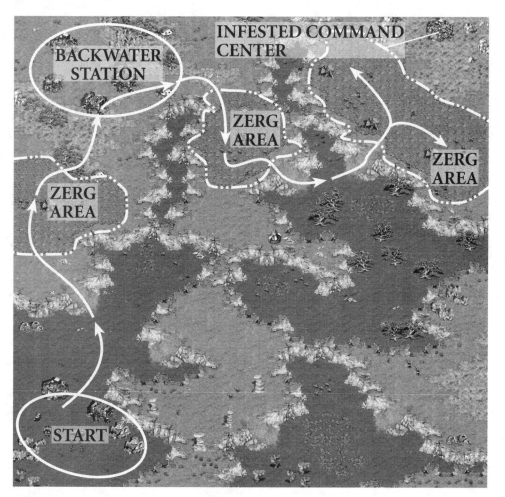

Fig. 4-4:

Map of Terran Mission 2.

Mission Overview

Backwater Station is under attack from unknown alien organisms. The Confederate headquarters on Tarsonis requests that you don't get involved, but Raynor is convinced the Confederate troops won't take action fast enough to save Backwater. It's risky, but if you team up with Raynor there's a chance you can get to Backwater Station before it's too late.

Mission Objectives

* Wipe out all Zerg structures.
* Raynor must survive.

Special Units

* Jim Raynor (in Vulture)

New Units

* Firebats

Enemy Units

* Zerglings
* Hydralisks

Battle Strategy

Your forces are grouped in the lower-left corner of the map, which gives you some measure of protection against the Zerg in the early going. After you've set up your SCVs to collect resources, set your Barracks to produce Marines until you have a squad of 12 ready to kick some Zergling butt. Take advantage of Jim Raynor's awesome power when you hunt Zerglings, and if he gets damaged, simply order an SCV to repair Jim's Vulture.

After you have 12 Marines, group them into one attack force and move northeast up the canyon to take out the few Zerglings waiting there. After their blood soaks the ground, move north up the ramp to slice up some Zerg. As soon as you climb the ramp you'll see the telltale sign of the Zerg's presence, called "Creep", as well as a Zerg structure guarded by a half-dozen Zerglings. Your 12 Marines will shred the Zerglings in the blink of an eye, leaving your firepower free to annihilate the Zerg structure.

Now move your group of Marines north until they capture the Backwater Station Command Center. When you get a unit close enough to the Center, all the other structures and units fall under your control, including two SCVs and five Firebats. Immediately order the two Barracks in Backwater to produce three or four Firebats each. Then park your Marines on the east (right) side of the station.

NOTE Think "blitzkrieg" when you attack with your Marines and Firebats in this mission. Don't hesitate to move into packs of Zerglings or Hydralisks. Your Marines are tougher than you may think, and before you know it you'll have crushed the Zerg.

Once you've created the Firebats, form another group made up entirely of these units. Now you have two groups—eight to 12 Marines (depending on how many have survived) and at least ten Firebats. Move your Marines southeast and have them take out any Hydralisks and Zerglings they encounter while the Firebat group follows up to destroy structures. This one-two punch is an effective tactic in these early missions, so keep moving throughout Zerg territory this way. The scenario ends when you destroy the infested Command Center. The infested Command Center lies in the upper-right corner of the map.

Resource Management

Begin by sending an SCV to build a Refinery on the Vespene Geyser to the north while your Command Center produces two more SCVs. Have the remaining SCV start harvesting minerals posthaste. Continue creating SCVs until you have six or seven of them, and leave all but one harvesting minerals. As minerals pour in, produce Marines until you have 12. That's it; that's all you have to do resource-wise to win this scenario. Your SCVs will continue collecting minerals while your lone Vespene Gas SCV slowly gives you all the gas you need to create Firebats down the road. This is a nice way to manage your resources in this mission, because basically you can set it up and forget it.

Fig. 4-5:

Once you have 12 Marines, go have some fun!

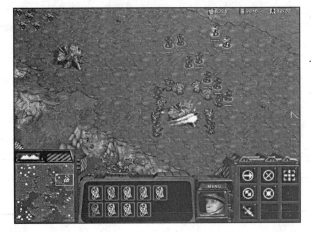

Fig. 4-6:

This is a very effective formation for the Terrans early on: Firebats in front, Marines in back.

MISSION #3:
DESPERATE ALLIANCE

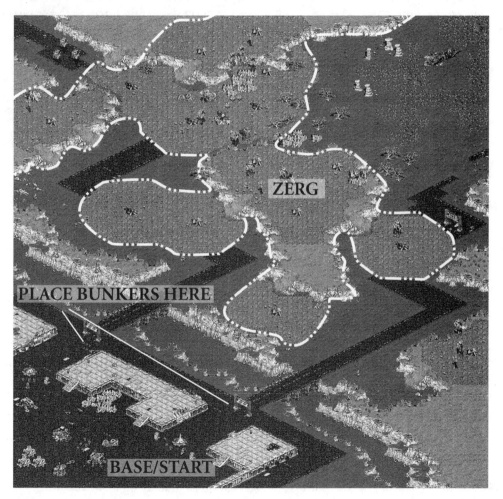

ZERG

PLACE BUNKERS HERE

BASE/START

Fig. 4-7:

Map of Terran Mission 3.

Mission Overview

Times are tough for the Terrans. The Confederation is failing to provide a cohesive resistance to the Zerg menace, and even more stations have fallen to Zerg forces. The Confederation has arrested many of the militia that otherwise would provide defense, and the only groups still available to fight are the right-wing factions. One such group is the Sons of Korhal, lead by Arcturus Mengsk. He has contacted you to request assistance in stemming the Zerg onslaught. However, should you join forces with Mengsk, you'll be branded a criminal.

Mission Objective

    * Survive for 30 minutes.

Special Units

    * None

New Unit

    * Vulture

Enemy Units

    * Zerglings
    * Hydralisks
    * Mutalisks
    * Overlords

Battle Strategy

Your objective in this scenario is to survive for 30 minutes, and there are a couple of ways to go about it. You can either build your defenses and sit tight, waiting for Zerg attackers to strike your position, or you can take an offensive stance and attempt to deal a blow to the Zerg before they come looking for trouble. The latter approach is more fun, and will give you some valuable experience managing an attack force.

First, you'll need to repair the burning Bunker on the lower road with an SCV. After that's done, throw the full complement of four Marines into each of your two Bunkers; this provides your base with a more than adequate defense as you build up your attack force.

Your attack force should consist of two (preferably three) groups of 12 Marines each, and one group of 12 Firebats. Upgrade Marine weapon range and armor strength before you set out. If all goes well, everything for your attack should be in place by minute 15. (You'll need extra Barracks to mobilize your army this quickly.)

**Fig. 4-8:**

Fix up this Bunker before you have to deal with another Zerg attack.

TIP Bunkers are incredibly powerful structures: They take the damage instead of your units, allowing you to defend an area against a large attack with only a few Marines. If you can, it's a good idea to keep an SCV around to repair Bunker damage. A Bunker with four Marines and a repair SCV can hold out a long time against seemingly insurmountable odds.

**Fig. 4-9:**

Once you have several groups of Marines and Firebats, come down on the Zerg, hard.

Group your units into groups of 12; then move then out en masse (Marines first, then Firebats) up the lower road. Begin a sweeping motion that systematically wipes out the heart of the Zerg Hive. Generally, Marines are your best weapons against Hydralisks and Mutalisks because they have greater range and their weapons penetrate Zerg armor better than Firebat weaponry.

Continue creating Marines at your base; you can use them as reinforcements if you need to. Remember, your objective is only to survive, not to obliterate the Zerg. If you launch this massive attack on Zerg positions, they'll have little chance to launch a counterattack. Now you can just let the clock tick toward victory if you want, but you should still stock your Bunkers with Marines. Just to be safe, keep a few extra emergency units (probably Marines) hanging around your base in case Mutalisks fly over. The key to this strategy is speed; if you are too slow the Zerg will have enough time to build a vast army.

NOTE

Counterpoint

If you don't feel aggressive, you can win this mission simply by building some extra Bunkers along the roads and stocking them with Firebats. Throw in a few extra Missile Turrets and a couple dozen Marines to guard the base, and you'll win without much trouble. Be sure to have at least three full Bunkers at each base entrance, as well as numerous Marines to handle flying enemies.

Resource Management

Your first concern is to get the greatest amount of minerals in the shortest period of time. Immediately set your Command Center to produce four new SCVs while the others collect minerals. After you've set six or seven SCVs collecting minerals, send one to repair the right-hand Bunker; then have it build a Refinery on the Vespene Geyser. You need no more than one SCV collecting Vespene; there should be enough to create the Firebats and upgrades you need.

At this point, produce a couple more SCVs to do some construction. Have one build Supply Depots and the other more Barracks. You'll need at least three new Supply Depots (four, if you choose to have four attack groups), so keep one SCV making Depots continually. You'll also need at least one SCV to repair damage from occasional Zerg attacks.

Before you know it, you'll have the Marine and Firebat groups ready for attack, and can simply leave your SCVs gathering minerals and Vespene while your Barracks produce more Marines. Go to it!

MISSION #4:
THE JACOBS INSTALLATION

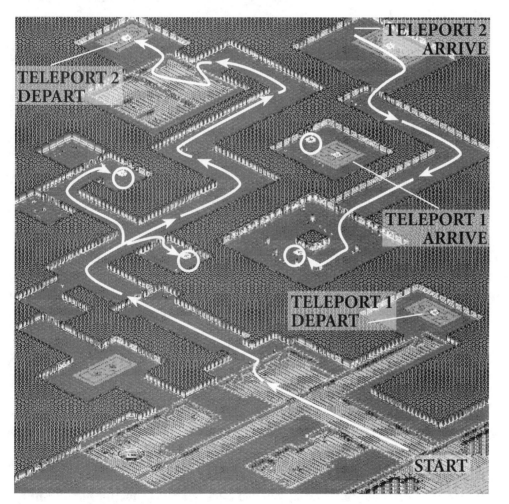

Fig. 4-10:

Map of Terran Mission 4.

TELEPORT 2
ARRIVE

TELEPORT 2
DEPART

TELEPORT 1
ARRIVE

TELEPORT 1
DEPART

START

Mission Overview

Your tenure as a Colonial Magistrate has been suspended pending an official investigation of your affiliation with the Sons of Korhal. The Zerg have overrun Mar Sara almost completely, and the Confederates are abandoning the planet. Mengsk wants you to raid Mar Sara's Confederate Outpost and bring back whatever designs or weapon schematics you can get your hands on in the Jacobs Installation.

Mission Objectives

* Retrieve data disks from the Confederate network.
* Bring disks back to the pickup point.
* Jim Raynor must survive.

Special Unit

* Jim Raynor

New Enemy Units (Terran)

* Floor-mounted guns (hidden)
* Wall-mounted guns (hidden)

Battle Strategy

Because this is an "installation" mission, the map is like a maze, and offers a number of superfluous pathways. Figure 4-10 shows the direct route through the installation. At several locations in this mission you'll encounter hidden floor and wall-mounted guns and Missile Turrets. Stay calm as you move through the installation and don't panic if the floor opens fire on you; simply target the spot and have your Marines destroy the turret.

As you move northwest you reach a room with a raised area serviced by three stairways. Several Marines and one Goliath defend this area, so don't head in there until you've grouped your attack force tightly. When you fight the Marines above you, remember that they have a height advantage. You have only a 70 percent chance of hitting them when you're lower, while they have a 100 percent chance of hitting you. Therefore, always attack when your numbers are at least three times theirs.

Be sure to activate any Beacons you come across as you wind through the installation. The first two Beacons you'll run across disable floor-mounted guns and release a number of friendly (and not-so-friendly) prisoners. The Third teleports your men so they can proceed along the optimal path and collect the disks. Once you grab the disks and return them to the starting Beacon, the mission will end in victory for you.

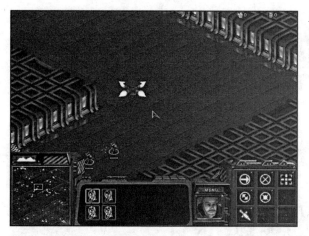

Fig. 4-11:

Watch out for wall- and floor-mounted guns in this mission.

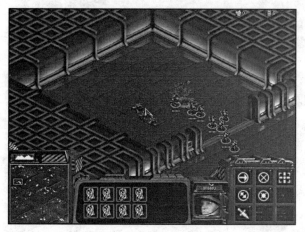

Fig. 4-12:

Group your Marines and Firebats, come down hard on the Zerg.

Resource Management

You can't build new units in this scenario, so take care not to waste units frivolously. If you end up losing a pile of units accidentally or due to a sloppy play, you may have to restart the scenario, so be very careful.

MISSION #5:

REVOLUTION

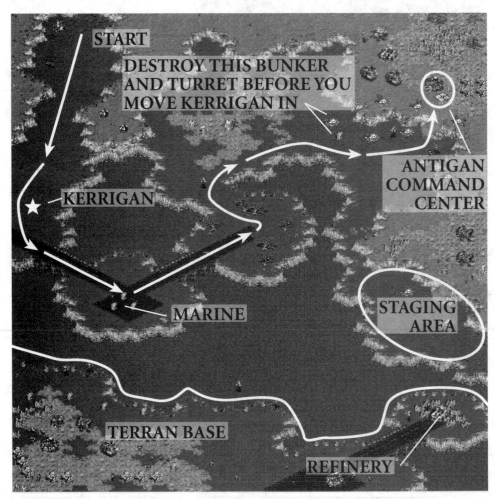

START

DESTROY THIS BUNKER
AND TURRET BEFORE YOU
MOVE KERRIGAN IN

**ANTIGAN
COMMAND
CENTER**

KERRIGAN

MARINE

**STAGING
AREA**

TERRAN BASE

REFINERY

Fig. 4-13:

Map of Terran Mission 5.

Mission Overview

With the disks secure, Raynor advises you that headquarters is analyzing the data and should have them decoded soon. Mengsk is confident your efforts have weakened the Confederate hold on the fringe worlds, but there's more work yet to be done. Sources have informed Kerrigan that the colony on Antiga Prime is ready to revolt against the Confederacy; however, a substantial group of Confederate troops (Alpha Squadron) is stationed around the colony. Kerrigan will help reclaim the colony, but you must use all your skills to eliminate the Confederate base established there.

Mission Objectives

* Take Kerrigan to the Confederate Command Center.
* Raynor and Kerrigan must survive.
* Destroy the Confederate base.

Special Units

* Jim Raynor (in Vulture)
* Kerrigan (Ghost)

New Units

* Wraith
* Dropship
* Vulture

Battle Strategy

This mission begins with your troops in the upper-left corner of the map. Group them and proceed south until you run into Kerrigan. After Kerrigan and Raynor engage in a brief verbal fencing match, proceed south until you reach the three Missile Turrets on the roadway. Destroy them. Continue along the road (now leading northeast) and take out the waiting Vulture.

The Confederate Wraith that stands in your way affords an excellent opportunity to use Kerrigan's Lockdown ability.

Next, turn north and head to a clearing just left of some Confederate Bunkers. Your Marines must take out a Confederate Wraith guarding this area, but otherwise you'll be safe there for a while. Separate Kerrigan from your group; then move your troops in to take out the Bunker directly to your right, and then the Missile Turret beside it. Missile Turrets are detectors and can see cloaked Ghosts, so you must take it out before you can sneak Kerrigan past.

Once the turret is gone, move your troops back; then cloak Kerrigan and move her up to the Beacon. With the turret destroyed, enemy units can't spot her when she's cloaked, so getting to the Beacons will be easy. After the Antigan base is liberated, the Antigan Bunkers will destroy most Confederate Forces near the base. You can move Raynor and the Marines in to mop up the last few Confederate Marines after the Confederate Bunkers succumb.

Fig. 4-14:

Take out this Bunker and Missile Turret to clear a path for Kerrigan.

After you liberate the Antigan base, your objective becomes destroying the Confederate base (that sprawls along the bottom of the map). You must get the Antigan base up and moving forward to generate the military *oomph* it will take to crush Alpha Squadron. Fortunately, the Antiga Prime base is substantial, and you needn't build a lot of infrastructure to win.

First, repair any buildings (or Jim Raynor's Vulture) that have taken damage; then set your Command Center to produce as many new SCVs as you can afford. After setting up your resource gathering, start producing Marines and Wraiths, as well as Missile Turrets, along the base's southern border. The Confederate base lies along the lower quarter of the map, so the best staging area for your attacks lies to the south.

Fig. 4-15:

Use Raynor to take out Confederate units that come knocking on the base doors.

Build up a strike force of 12 Wraiths (with cloaking ability and Apollo Reactors), and 12 or so Marines with upgraded weapons and armor (if possible). Then get ready to mix it up. Cloak your Wraiths and head to the lower-right portion of the map, where a Confederate Refinery and plenty of SCVs rush resources back to the Command Center. As your cloaked Wraiths fire on the SCVs and Refinery, many Confederate Wraiths will fly in to stop the carnage; because your ships are cloaked, you can lay waste to them quickly.

NOTE **The Power of the Cloaked Wraith**

A large group of cloaked Wraiths can wreak havoc on enemy air and ground units. As long as you're careful to back up your Wraiths with ground units that can take out detector units such as Missile Turrets (Terran) or Spore Colonies (Zerg), the Wraiths can turn the tide of a battle.

Fig. 4-16:

Use a combination of cloaked Wraiths and Marines to sweep through the Confederation base.

After clearing the lower-right map corner of the Confederate menace, load the Dropship with Marines and transport them to the secured area. Move as many as you can; then collect them into one or two groups. Now you'll move from east to west across the bottom of the map with your Wraiths and Marines. There may be Spider Mines in this area; send lone Marines ahead of your main attack force to detonate them. Use your cloaked Wraiths to take out air and ground units while your Marines move forward to knock out Missile Turrets that would give your Wraiths' position away. Using this method, you'll quickly sweep the Confederate base off the map, leaving only a few straggling units for your Wraiths to hunt down.

Resource Management

After capturing the Antigan Base, your goal is to quickly amass a small army of SCVs to collect the large amounts of minerals and Vespene you'll need to construct the necessary Wraiths. After liberating the base, set the Command Center to build five SCVs while the two active SCVs collect minerals and repair damage to Jim Raynor and any buildings that took hits during the fighting.

Once the resource gathering is in full swing, build several new Supply Depots to accommodate the strike force. You also must build a Comsat Station so you can develop Cloaking, and an Engineering Bay to build Missile Turrets to protect the base from Confederate Wraith attacks. You may want to move your Starport down to the lower part of the map, but it also can be beneficial to build a second Starport at the southern portion of the base. If you are enterprising, you can build a Command Center in the south to help speed up the Vespene Gas collection.

MISSION #6:
NORAD II

Fig. 4-17:

Map of Terran Mission 6.

Mission Overview

The Confederation is in shock over the Antigan revolt. The remains of Alpha Squadron, and its commander, General Duke, have crash-landed in their flagship, *Norad II*. It's your job to move in and save the colony—and Duke, as well. It's a bitter pill for Raynor and Kerrigan to swallow, but Mengsk feels saving Duke will make him a powerful ally. War is hell.

Mission Objectives

✳ Protect Battlecruiser *Norad II*.

✳ Take Raynor to *Norad II*.

Special Unit

✳ Jim Raynor (in Vulture)

New Units

✳ Goliath

New Enemy Units

✳ Mutalisk

✳ Spore Colony

Battle Strategy

Your base is in disarray following a Zerg attack, and several of your buildings will need repair. Your first priority is to mobilize Raynor (in his Vulture) and the Marines and Firebats around him to secure the base. While you're moving your Marines into the existing bunkers, use your SCVs to fix up any buildings that are terminally damaged (in the red zone). If a building that is in the red zone is not repaired, it will eventually explode and be lost.

Fig. 4-18:

First things first: Take out this Sunken Colony and the Zerglings hitting your structures.

Terminal Buildings

If a Terran building has taken enough damage to put it into the red zone, it will continue deteriorating until it's been destroyed. Once a building reaches this state, you must repair it at least to the yellow level to avoid losing the structure.

Norad II Strategy

When the Norad II comes online, you'll notice that you have a pair of SCVs and some other units (Goliaths, Marines and Firebats). This position will undergo fairly heavy Zerg attacks in the early part of this mission, so repair any Bunker damage you may have taken. Then, put your units (including the SCVs) into the Bunkers. As the enemy swarms attack, your Bunkers will take a beating, but, whenever they need to be repaired you can simply pop one of your SCVs out of the Bunker to fix it, and then pop it back in.

During quiet periods (when the Norad II isn't under attack), use your SCVs to repair the ship. However, always keep a look out for enemy attacks; your SCVs are too valuable to lose them. Whatever you do, don't attempt to build any units near Norad II, and don't attempt to launch any attacks from this position. If you do, you'll bring the wrath of the Zerg down upon you, and the mission will be over.

After thwarting the initial Zerg attack, there's only a short period of time for you to get your defenses back up before the next onslaught. Continue repairing damaged structures while you put Marines (and/or Firebats) into the existing Bunkers. If you can spare the resources, build another Bunker near the Refinery to protect your north flank.

Once you have a defense perimeter of Marine-filled Bunkers, you'll have a shield Zerg ground attacks can't penetrate. Your next priority is to build up a fleet of Wraiths and a large contingent (20) of Vultures, Goliaths, and Marines to mount an assault on the Spore Colonies guarding the airways between the base and the *Norad II*.

Fig. 4-19:

Build up a solid strike force to hit the Zerg Spore Colonies hard.

CAUTION With the resources at your fingertips in this scenario, you may be tempted to try to take out all the Zerg by force. That could be suicide. The Zerg you can't see—the ones just east and north of the Norad II—are numerous, and defeating them would take a very long time. In this case, it's better to be sneaky than ruthless.

Once your troops are ready to go, move the Dropships to the edge of the ridge east of your base. There's one area where the Spore Colonies can't hit your ships, but you may still want to throw a Wraith or two out front to take hits instead of your Dropships. Once your troops are up on the ledge, move systematically from one Spore Colony to the next, clearing an area for a Dropship to come through. At this point, expect the Zerg to throw plenty of Mutalisis and some ground units at you; you should have your Wraiths ready for backup.

Fig. 4-20:

After clearing the path, bring Raynor to the Beacon by way of a Dropship.

As this battle goes on, send one Dropship back for reinforcements (any mix of units you prefer) and the other to pick up Jim Raynor. When you're fairly sure you can sneak a Dropship to the *Norad II,* fly it in and drop Raynor onto the Beacon.

That's it. You win.

Resource Management

The most precious resources to manage at the beginning of this mission are the buildings that have fallen into the red zone. They'll collapse in minutes (or seconds) if you don't get an SCV over to do some repair work. After securing the area and ensuring you won't lose buildings to deterioration, build six to ten SCVs to start gathering resources. Devote one SCV exclusively to repairing damaged buildings and constructing Bunkers.

After this tense initial period, you can gather resources in a business-as-usual manner, making sure you build a Starport with a Control Tower, and an Engineering Bay so you can make Wraiths and Missile Turrets as the game progresses. Whatever your plan, you should use your resources first to repair structures and provide a defensive curtain around your base and then to make Wraiths and Goliaths.

MISSION #7:
THE TRUMP CARD

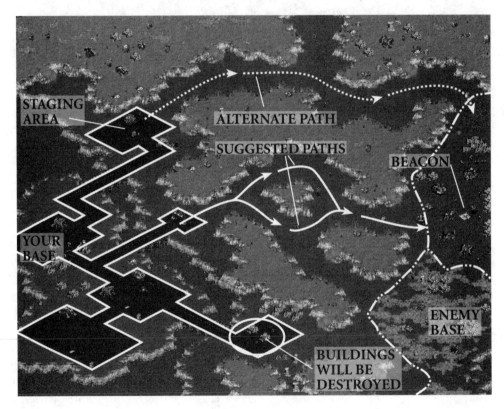

Fig. 4-21:

Map of Terran Mission 7.

Mission Overview

A large Confederate strike force readies to attack your position. That's not the big news, however. You learn the Confederation has developed a Trans-planar Psionic Waveform Emitter. When activated, this Psi Emitter attracts Zerg to its location: As it turns out, a Psi Emitter was at the heart of the battle on Mar Sara. It may seem like a cruel strike against your race, but your only option is to plant a Psi Emitter in the Command Center of the Confederation camp, leaving the Confederates to deal with the Zerg while you escape.

Mission Objectives

* Bring the Psi Emitter to the enemy base.
* Kerrigan must survive.

Special Unit

* Kerrigan (Ghost)

New Units

* Siege Tank
* Science Vessel

New Enemy Unit (Terran)

* Siege Tank

Battle Strategy

As soon as this mission starts you must pull back some of your units and buildings. The area in the lower-middle part of the map probably will be destroyed before you can help it, and the area at the top of the map (where Kerrigan and the Psi Emitter are) also come under attack quickly. Let the lower area fall, but try to hang onto the northern camp to use as a staging area for your attacks. Launch the Science Facility and the Spaceport, and move them south (out of range of the enemy Bunkers). Immediately send up reinforcements from your main base for defense.

To reach the Beacon (where you must drop the Psi Emitter), you must punch a hole in Confederate defenses. You can use two routes for this—the central path and the northern path leading from your northern staging area. Either way, a fair bit of fighting must occur, but because fewer Missile Turrets guard the northern route it allows for better use of Wraith fighters for attack.

Fig. 4-22:

Expect to lose these Supply Depots and Bunker to Siege Tank attacks before you even know what's happening.

Build up a force of about 10 Siege Tanks, 12 Wraiths, 10 Goliaths, and 12 Marines. Then move systematically along the northern corridor. It's a good idea to send your Science Vessel ahead of your other troops to warn you of waiting Siege Tanks. Creep forward using a systematic pattern of Goliaths and Marines followed closely by Siege Tanks, with the Wraiths nearby for backup. Bring a couple of SCVs to repair damage to your units along the way.

Distraction Works

As you begin your move up the northern corridor, you may want to send a couple of Goliaths or Siege Tanks up the central pathway to distract Confederation forces. Doing this can occupy part of the enemy troops, making your job in the north that much easier.

Remember to use ground units, such as Goliaths and Marines, to take out Turrets, Wraiths, and Siege Tanks. When you come to the mineral field at the top of the Confederate base, take out all the SCVs and the Command Center to cripple the Confederate ability to create more units. Then move your Siege Tanks into the center of town. Once these tanks enter "siege mode" the carnage really begins, and enemy structures fall very quickly. At this point, get the Psi Emitter into a Dropship to fly it up to the Beacon. Fly the Dropship along the pathway your ground forces cleared; otherwise, Missile Turrets may shoot it down.

Drop the Psi Emitter (transported by an SCV) near the Beacon; then move it in. The mission ends with Kerrigan wishing that she is never forced to contribute to human death again by luring Zerg to attack.

Fig. 4-23:

Move your forces up the corridor in groups of Goliaths and Marines, Siege Tanks, and Wraiths.

Fig. 4-24:

When you can park a couple of Siege Tanks in the Confederate base, the end is near.

Resource Management

As with most missions, it's important to start collecting minerals and Vespene Gas as soon as possible. Use some of your initial minerals to create a pair of new SCVs to help. Balance your need for new military units with your need for new structures (such as a Machine Shop for the Factory and more Supply Depots).

It may be advisable to build another Factory and/or Barracks in the northern staging area, but if the resources are hard to find, simply move your existing structures north to keep fresh units flowing to the front. Once your strike force is ready, keep building units at your base(s) so you can send in another wave of firepower if it looks like you're losing the battle.

MISSION #8:
THE BIG PUSH

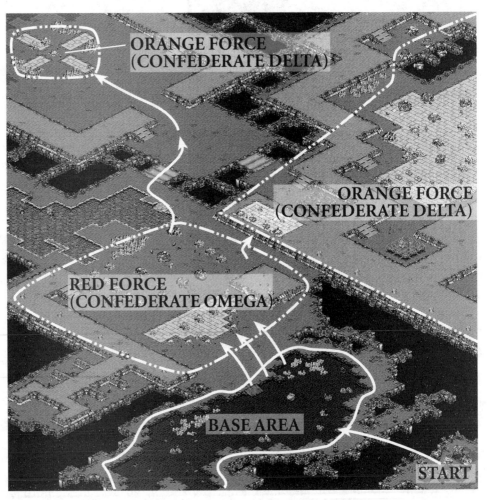

ORANGE FORCE
(CONFEDERATE DELTA)

ORANGE FORCE
(CONFEDERATE DELTA)

RED FORCE
(CONFEDERATE OMEGA)

BASE AREA

START

Fig. 4-25:

Map of Terran Mission 8.

Mission Overview

It's nearly time to take out the Confederate base at Tarsonis, but to break through defenses you must plan carefully. General Duke has devised a plan to attack the central of the three primary orbiting platforms. These platforms serve as staging areas for the Confederate fleet, so a sufficient attack on one should cause enough of a panic to allow a small force of troops to penetrate to the planet surface.

Mission Objectives

* Eliminate the Confederate Forces.
* Duke must survive.

Special Unit

* Duke (Battlecruiser with Yamato Gun)

New Units

* Battlecruiser
* Ghost
* Nuke

Battle Strategy

As this mission begins, all your troops are crammed onto a small platform, along with all your buildings (which are hovering). Load your SCVs and Marines into Dropships. Then group the Wraiths with Duke and move them left to the deserted base. Once there, have your air force take out the Confederate Marines and Firebats dotting the area. It shouldn't take much to clean them up.

Move your structures to the new base, placing your Command Centers between mineral fields and Vespene Geysers. You can drop your buildings beside add-on buildings such as Machine Shops and Nuclear Missile Silos for instant upgrades. Immediately get your SCVs gathering minerals while you create Siege Tanks and Marines.

Fig. 4-26:

Take advantage of the structures Alpha Squadron left behind.

After you've sorted out what buildings go where, move your air units to the raised area above your base. You can also add a few Bunkers and any Siege Tanks you create, so they'll be in place for your slow, grinding assault across the central portion of the map.

Fig. 4-27:

Use the Yamato Gun to disable the Missile Turrets protecting the Confederate bases.

Yamato Gun

The Yamato Gun on Duke's Battlecruiser is a devastating weapon that can take out a Missile Turret in one hit. It also can do enough damage to a building with one hit that the building (if Terran) will degrade and eventually explode. It's an impressive weapon that can make your life much easier. Many use the Yamato Gun as just a Turret Killer, but it can be much more.

Build up your forces as you did in the last mission—three large groups of Siege Tanks, Goliaths/Marines, and Wraiths. Move these groups up the central and left portions of the map where you can capture vast mineral and Vespene deposits. If you build Command Centers near these new deposits, you can speed up your defeat of the Confederates.

This is the first mission where you get to use Nukes, and if you build plenty of Command Centers around the extra mineral deposits, you can have extra silos (and therefore extra Nukes). Several Confederate installations on this map have closely grouped buildings—perfect targets for the awesome power of a nuclear device. Use a cloaked Ghost to get in close to a target; then let the Nuke go. If you can follow up with a mop-up force, you can take out entire bases in a short period of time. Still, you don't need to use nukes to win the mission. A slow assault with Siege Tanks and support forces works just as well.

Using Nukes

Use a Ghost to move close to a target, then select the Nuke and you'll notice that target is "painted" with a laser beam (a red dot). It takes about 10-15 seconds for the Nuke to hit, so keep your Ghost cloaked.

Fig. 4-28:

Nukes are most effective when the enemy has plenty of units and structures closely grouped together.

After you capture other mineral deposits and knock out the first Confederate base on the platform, the others will fall with help from Siege Tanks and Nukes. This mission can take quite awhile, but you'll have fun. After you take the base just above your own, most of the Confederate Forces lie entirely along the right(east) side of the map.

Resource Management

The key to winning this mission is to secure the mineral fields and Vespene resource pools above and on the left (west) side of the map. Building Command Centers near these areas to help rake in more resources is critical if you want to win by overwhelming the Confederate Forces.

MISSION #9:
NEW GETTYSBERG

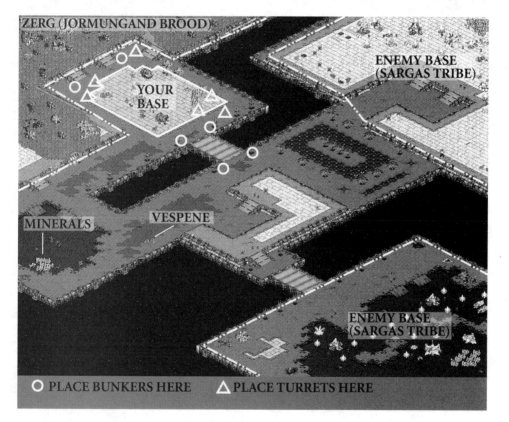

ZERG (JORMUNGAND BROOD)

YOUR BASE

ENEMY BASE (SARGAS TRIBE)

MINERALS

VESPENE

ENEMY BASE (SARGAS TRIBE)

○ PLACE BUNKERS HERE   △ PLACE TURRETS HERE

Fig. 4-29:

Map of Terran Mission 9.

Mission Overview

Intelligence tells us the Protoss are descending on the Zerg Hive on Tarsonis. Mengsk worries the Protoss will divert the Zerg from their attacks on the Confederation, and has ordered Kerrigan to engage the Protoss forces so the Zergs can be unencumbered in their attacks on the Confederation.

Mission Objectives

* Destroy Protoss force.
* All Zerg buildings must survive.
* Kerrigan must survive.

Special Unit

* Kerrigan (Ghost)

New Unit

* Battlecruiser (standard)

New Enemy Units (Protoss)

* Dragoon
* Zealot
* Scout
* Shuttle

Battle Strategy

A large force of Zerg lies just north of your position; however, you can't attack the Zerg actively because destroying even one Zerg building will result in mission failure. Instead, you must place Bunkers (filled with Marines) near the ramps leading up to Zerg positions. As resources allow, also place a few Missile Turrets in the area to protect against Mutalisk attack. In fact, placing these defensive structures along the northern boundary of your base should be your first priority. Once they're in place they'll do their work without your attention.

Send your Dropship with some SCVs to claim the mineral deposits in the left-center and bottom-center portions of the map. Then build an Armory, a Starport, a Refinery (if you haven't yet), and a Science Station. As this is going on, build a pair of Bunkers on the path behind the mineral field at your base. The Protoss eventually will send Zealots through this area, and if you don't have a pair of well-stocked Bunkers you'll get toasted.

Fig. 4-30

Build up a good defense network so the Zerg to the north won't bother you as you fight the Protoss.

NOTE **Zealots**

These units look like the equivalent of Marines, but in fact they're much tougher to kill, and their attacks have more than twice the power of a Marine's gun. Although they look like you can match up one on one with Marines or Firebats, doing so will mean a one way ticket to Bloodville.

You can attempt to win this mission through a bloody ground-based battle, but an alternative strategy will save your troops' lives. However, it will cost you plenty of resources. After setting up your two new Command Centers and protecting the main base sufficiently, build an extra Starport, making sure to include a Control Tower. Once you can build Battlecruisers, build them as fast as you can until you have eight or ten. This is no small task, and you must defend your base against Protoss attacks as you amass this force. It will be worth it in the end, however.

Fig. 4-31:

When you have a fleet of Battlecruisers, get ready to knock the stuffing out of the Protoss.

Once you have the fleet of Battlecruisers, fly them down to your lower Control Center and make sure you've researched the Yamato Gun. Finally, before you begin your attack, group four to six SCVs as a repair team that can repair badly damaged Battlecruisers quickly. Use your Comsat Stations to locate enemy Photon Cannons; then move your fleet of Battlecruisers in for the kill. Work your way along the bottom of the map until you've wiped out all the structures. If you're getting clobbered, return to base for repair.

Battlecruiser Priorities

Before you move a large fleet of Battlecruisers into battle, remember to prioritize the units you'll attack. Photon Cannons, Dragoons, and Scouts, which fire back, take priority over shuttles or other buildings. If you mobilize the entire fleet's firepower on one of these units, often you can destroy them in one volley, so often it's wise to focus on one unit at a time. The remaining structures can wait until you've eliminated the most threatening units.

Fig. 4-32:

As you wreak havoc on the Protoss bases, don't rule out the possibility of a large Zerg offensive: Keep your defenses up.

As you work your way through the Protoss base, don't be afraid to use your Yamato Guns to take out larger structures. Most structures will succumb after two Yamato shots; use this weapon together with the other Battlecruisers' lasers to go through the base like a hot knife through butter. The remaining Protoss structures lie in the upper-right corner of the map. Go to it.

Resource Management

Once your base is secure from random Zerg attacks, use your Dropship to take two SCVs down to the mineral deposits in the left-center and bottom-center areas of the map. Next, build Command Centers near the mineral fields as quickly as possible. This speeds up this mission considerably. The mineral field at the bottom-center of the map is close to a large Protoss installation, so don't venture far. Just build the Command Center and start collecting minerals.

This scenario has a fixed amount of resources, and long, drawn-out battles will surely deplete what you'd otherwise need for a decisive victory. Don't fritter away your resources during the build-up phase, and don't attack until you have at least eight Battlecruisers. For best results, gather all the resources you can—as quickly as you can— as you build the structures you need to create Battlecruisers.

MISSION #10:
The Hammer Falls

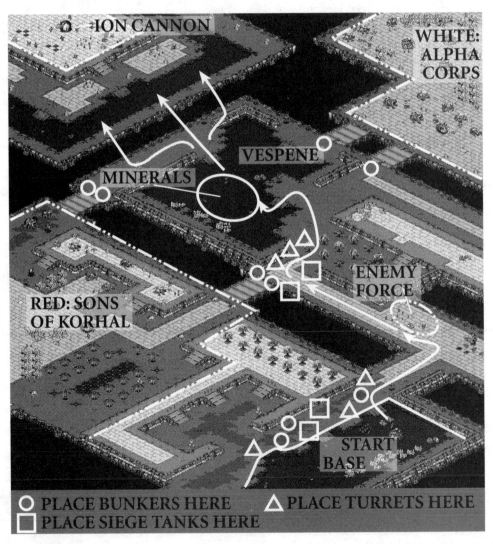

ION CANNON

WHITE:
ALPHA
CORPS

VESPENE

MINERALS

ENEMY
FORCE

RED: SONS
OF KORHAL

START
BASE

○ **PLACE BUNKERS HERE**   △ **PLACE TURRETS HERE**
□ **PLACE SIEGE TANKS HERE**

Fig. 4-33:
Map of Terran Mission 10.

Mission Overview

The fleet has lost contact with the ground forces at New Gettysberg. General Mengsk has ordered the immediate disengagement of the Korhal fleet from the Tarsonian system. Meanwhile, Protoss and Zerg forces continue battling across the core continent of Tarsonis. Raynor is bitter about Mengsk's betrayal of Kerrigan and is set to abandon Mengsk and his self-centered plans for conquest. Mengsk threatens to destroy anyone who opposes him, but Raynor (and you) are ready to leave Tarsonis as soon as possible. The fleet is ready to evacuate you, but you must disable an Ion Cannon before the fleet can leave.

Mission Objectives

* Destroy the Tarsonis Ion Cannon.
* Raynor must survive.

Special Unit

* Raynor (in Vulture)

New Enemy Units

* Science Vessel

Battle Strategy

There are two main groups of enemy Terrans in this mission—the Sons of Korhal (red) and the Alpha Corps (white). The red force, which has troops stationed on and behind the raised area directly north of your starting position, poses the immediate threat to you. Providing a proper defensive barrier should be your first priority, so build Bunkers and Missile Turrets in the area at the top of the ramps. Take care not to wander too far or the Siege Tanks just out of your range will smoke you.

**Fig. 4-34:**

Bunker up your northern flank right away to avoid the red menace.

After securing the area, build a pack of 12 Marines and group them together; then grab your two Siege Tanks and head down the road to the right. At the intersection you'll encounter a group of red Goliaths and Marines, but they should be no problem for your Marines. After you've secured this area, quickly move north to the next intersection and build a pair of Bunkers blocking the road to the left. The red forces will attack along this route from both the air and the ground, so it would behoove you to put a couple Missile Turrets here to spot cloaked Wraiths.

Fig. 4-35:

Build plenty of Missile Turrets to protect your new property from air attacks.

What you're doing is essentially blocking off key attack access points for the red force. Defending these two areas well will prevent any red attacks from breaking through. You now have access to a pair of large resource deposits (see figure 4-33 for their locations). These will give you the power you need to take out the Ion Cannon.

The enemy won't take lightly your setting up Command Centers near these newly discovered mineral fields, and will likely launch waves of Wraiths (capable of cloaking) at them. To prevent your excursions from becoming disasters, build Missile Turrets around each Command Center. These will serve both to shoot down enemy airborne units and to spot cloaked Wraiths. If you fail to block off all enemy paths of attack, you can still win. Just make sure you establish a strong presence somewhere near the central resources and start packing the area with Bunkers, Missile Turrets, Goliaths, and Siege Tanks in Siege Mode. The enemy will throw a surprising variety of enemies from all directions, so you'll need to constantly build new units. Build new Barracks and Factories to speed up unit production in the area.

If victory seems impossible, start over and this time try to spread into the central resource area faster. Once you've gotten there, don't stop building defenses until the area is completely blanketed. This is the hardest part of the mission; once you've established yourself in that central area, started harvesting resources, and started cranking out Battlecruisers, you've practically won. Turn down game speed if things get too hectic.

Fig. 4-36:

The Ion Cannon is well-defended, and it will take a strong attack force to break through.

After securing these areas, begin to build a strong strike force of Battlecruisers, Wraiths, Science Vessels, Dropships, and, of course, the entire gamut of ground units. To take out the Ion Cannon, you must move your Battlecruisers in first to destroy the Missile Turrets at the edge of the platform. Once these have been neutralized, you can either land Dropships in the clear spot or proceed with your fleet of Battlecruisers and slowly annihilate all resistance. If you've managed to develop a fleet of at least five Battlecruisers with Yamato Guns, this latter approach is much easier. Just advance the Battlecrusiers very slowly, using Scanner Sweeps to reveal Ghosts and Yamato Guns to level Missile Turrets. Eventually you'll reach the Ion Cannon. Destroy it with the Battlecruisers and victory is yours.

Resource Management

After you've secured the new mineral fields in the northeast, you must research the technologies to their fullest. Fortunately, with the new mineral deposits you'll have plenty of resources to upgrade every aspect of your units' abilities. Once the defensive infrastructure is in place, pour your efforts into building the strike force. The sooner you can take the Ion Cannon out, the less chance the enemy will launch a large attack on one of your positions, draining your resource pool.

Chapter 5:

THE
ZERG
MISSIONS

MISSION #1:
AMONG THE RUINS

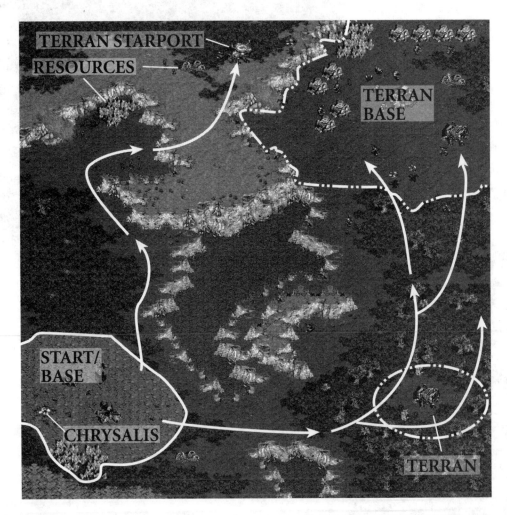

TERRAN STARPORT
RESOURCES
TERRAN BASE
START/ BASE
CHRYSALIS
TERRAN

Fig. 5-1:

Map of Zerg Mission 1.

Mission Overview

The Overmind has set you as one of the greatest of the Cerebrates. The Overmind has found a creature that is perhaps the greatest of his agents, and charges you with the task of keeping this Chrysalis safe from alien attacks, while you wipe the sector clean of the Terran menace that infests the planet nearby.

Mission Objectives

* Protect the Chrysalis.
* Destroy Terrans.

Special Unit

* Chrysalis

New Units

* Zergling
* Hydralisk

Battle Strategy

This mission is a giant leap down in difficulty from the last scenario (Terran Mission 10), but you're learning to use a new race, so the reprieve will be welcome. The solution here can be summed up in one word: Hydralisk. Follow the natural progression of technological advancement and then build 20 Hydralisks to crush the inferior Terran race.

This mission will give you a feel for the Zerg ground units: the Zergling and the Hydralisk. You can produce them quickly and cheaply, and the Hydralisk packs surprising power against everything from Wraiths to Goliaths. The key to this mission that is worthy of special attention is the Chrysalis. Keep a group of at least six Zerglings nearby at all times to protect this special unit from Terran attacks. It's also a good idea to build at least a pair of Sunken Colonies near the Chrysalis. The enemy will attack along the ground and the Sunken Colonies will provide an extra measure of support in case you get overwhelmed.

Fig. 5-2:

Keep a defensive force of Zerglings around your Hatchery and Chrysalis in case of surprise Terran attacks.

After building up two groups of 12 Zerglings and Hydralisks each, move up the right side of the map and take out the installations you come across. Use your Hydralisks to blast Wraiths from the sky while your Zerglings tie up attacking ground units. After you reach the main base, the attack force probably will be down 50 percent—a good indication that you should bring up another group of units. If you haven't produced them yet, Zerglings are quick and come two to an egg.

Fig. 5-3:

Find out what it's like to see Zerglings swarm Terran troops.

The only other area you must clear is in the upper-middle portion of the map, but you can approach it only from the left. A Starport and some light resistance await you there. Once you've swept the Terrans away, you win.

Resource Management

Although much Zerg resource management resembles that of the Terrans, you need to know a few key things before you venture forth. First, whenever you create a new structure, you lose the Drone that created it. That's because the Drone mutates into the structure—becomes it rather than builds it. Drones that have built a structure aren't free to do something else. They're gone forever.

In this scenario (as in most) you should create as many Drones as possible early on and build a Spawning Pool and a Hydralisk Den. An Evolution Chamber will help strengthen your weapons, but it's not necessary. However, you should explore new technologies to their fullest in every mission. Being comfortable with the methods and powers of each unit and structure will benefit you later in the game and in multi-player battles.

For fun, you can create swarms of Zerglings just to see what it's like to attack in such large (albeit weak) numbers. Remember, the Overlords are equivalent to Terran Supply Depots; if you plan to create a huge throng of Zerglings, have Overlords ready.

MISSION #2:
Egression

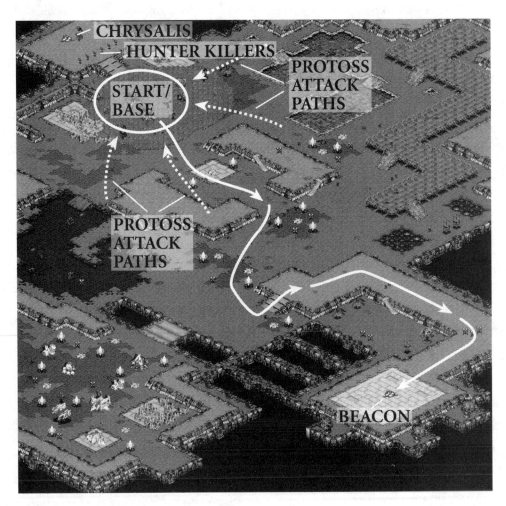

CHRYSALIS

HUNTER KILLERS

PROTOSS
ATTACK
PATHS

START/
BASE

PROTOSS
ATTACK
PATHS

BEACON

Fig. 5-4:

Map of Zerg Mission 2.

Mission Overview

The Overmind is pleased that its prize (the Chrysalis) is intact. You're considered strong enough now to engage in warp travel with the Swarm. The Protoss block your exit from Tarsonis, so must fight your way through to the Beacon to warp with the Swarm to a new destination. Another Cerebrate's Brood will help you if you need assistance during this mission.

Mission Objectives

* Take the Chrysalis to the Beacon.

Special Units

* Hunter Killer
* Chrysalis

New Units

* Scourge
* Mutalisk

New Enemy Units (Protoss)

* Dragoon
* Zealot

Battle Strategy

Your fellow Cerebrate has given you the use of six Hunter Killers. These units are essentially double-power Hydralisks and will aid you greatly in taking out the Protoss lying between you and the Beacon. Send a unit to the Hunter Killers to activate them. Immediately you have a force of six Hunter Killers and three Hydralisks. These nine units are strong enough to take out the entire initial string of Protoss structures and units. Move forward and attack, but as soon as you start losing units, fall back and nurse your wounds.

 Don't move off the Creep until you are ready to keep your attention on your attacks. It's probably a good idea to build five or six extra Hydralisks before you attack the Protoss if you're unsure of your tactics.

Fig. 5-5:

Use your strong initial force of Hunter Killers and Hydralisks to take out the immediate Protoss threat.

As your resources grow, you'll gain the ability to mutate Hydralisks. Make as many of these units as you can so you can have two large groups of Hydralisks (some will be Hunter Killers) that you can move through the map. After setting up this force, move them down toward the Beacon (in the lower-right corner of the map) destroying enemy units you meet along the way.

Tactics with Large Groups

When playing as the Zerg, often you'll find yourself managing large groups of units at once. Simply letting them go won't put you in the winner's circle. Instead, you must group your units carefully and issue new attack orders after every kill. Often a group of 12 units can destroy a single enemy unit in one collective shot. If you can move such group attacks quickly from one unit to another you can take out powerful enemies with few casualties. Let them fight one-on-one, however, and you could lose them all.

Fig. 5-6:

Be aggressive in your attacks. Taking a cavalier attitude during a hot-and-heavy battle can result in plenty of dead Zerg.

If your units falter, build more Hydralisks and/or Zerglings to replace your losses; then quickly send them into action. Soon you'll secure the Beacon. Now, rather than have a Drone bring the Chrysalis down unprotected, send a group of Hydralisks to escort the Drone to the Beacon.

Resource Management

As the mission begins, set two of your Drones to collect minerals while the third mutates into a Vespene Extractor. Again, try to exploit the Hydralisk's power by building a Hydralisk Den and then upgrading its weapons and movement numbers. Resource-gathering in this mission is routine, but be sure to leave some units behind in case the Protoss launch a counterattack (which they're known to do).

MISSION #3:
The New Dominion

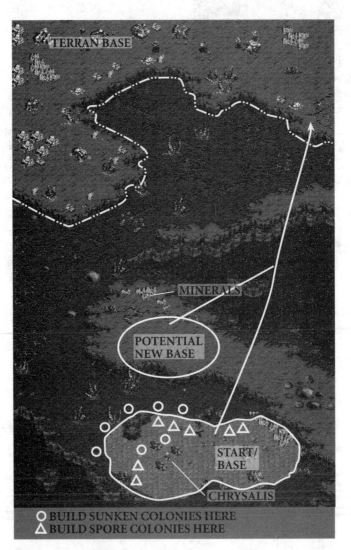

Fig. 5-7:

Map of Zerg Mission 3.

Mission Overview

The Chrysalis's psionic emanations have lured the enemy to us from the depths of space. We have intercepted a Terran transmission, and we know now there will be Terran forces chasing our Swarms. Engage the Terrans with care. Your priorities are first to protect the Chrysalis at all costs, and then to destroy the Terrans.

Mission Objectives

✳ Protect the Chrysalis.
✳ Eliminate the Terran presence.

Special Unit

✳ Chrysalis

Battle Strategy

Quickly building up a strong attack force will let you take the high ground to your north, speeding this mission along. You'll also want to set up a Sunken Colony on the upper-left edge of the Creep to defend against Terran attack (and they *will* attack).

Fig. 5-8:

The Terrans will be coming, so prepare with some ground units and Sunken Colonies.

After setting up a defensive perimeter, start producing Mutalisks and Hydralisks in bulk (the Mutalisks are more important). The sooner you can amass at least 10 Mutalisks, the better. Use your large group of Mutalisks to clear the high ground to your north (in the center of the map) so you can build a Hatchery and harvest the minerals and Vespene resources there.

Expect at least a couple of waves of Terran attacks, all from the left side of your base. Generally, your large group(s) of Mutalisks can stop any of these attacks, but you also should keep three or four Hydralisks and a Sunken Colony or two active around your base just to be safe.

Fig. 5-9:

Don't underestimate the power of a large group of any unit. In this case, Mutalisks can dominate the mission with relative ease.

Once you have two groups of 20 Mutalisks (ten in each group), keep building more to replace those you'll lose; then head up the map, aggressively confronting enemy Missile Turrets and Marines (the main threats to your Mutalisks). You'll take some hits, but the power of 12 Mutalisks focused together against one area is awesome. Turrets fall in a matter of seconds, getting only two or three shots off before becoming rubble. As your Mutalisks fall, fly replacements up to keep the strike force at around ten units or so. You can sweep the Terrans off the map, and enjoy doing it.

If you're having trouble cracking the Terran defensive perimeter, attack with your Mutalisks in the upper right corner of the map. This is where the Terrans are the weakest, and it'll be all you can do to gain a foothold on their territory. Be wary of marching ground troops north because the Terran Siege Tanks will obliterate anything in seconds. Use your Mutalisks to take the Siege Tanks out first. Lastly, if you run into large groups of Marines, back off and beef up your attack force or you may get shredded.

Resource Management

Begin by creating three new Drones while you set the two existing Drones to collecting minerals. Then ramp up production as fast as possible. Building a Sunken Colony near the Chrysalis should be a priority. Considering the ferocity of potential Terran attacks, it would behoove you quickly to get a second in place, as well.

After you're established, put all your resources into a Mutalisk strike force that can clear the mineral and Vespene area to the north. Once you have this area you can produce offensive units very quickly with two active Hatcheries.

Fig. 5-12:

Use a strong force of Mutalisks to neutralize the Terran Missile Turrets before you attempt a ground-unit landing.

MISSION #4:
AGENT OF THE SWARM

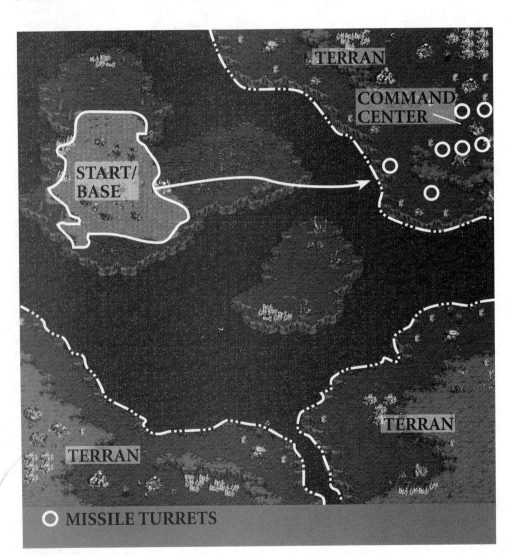

When you first begin your aerial assault, bring your ships in two waves, with the first wave taking the Missile Turrets quickly, and then the second wave to attack miscellaneous ground units, such as Marines and Goliaths. Mutalisks are good for these kinds of targets because their attacks bounce from one enemy unit to another, inflicting collateral damage on adjacent units. After the Missile Turrets have been destroyed, you can bring in your Queen and infest the Command Center to win the mission.

If you don't like the idea of an all-out air attack, you'll need to research Overlord Transport and pack up some Zerglings and Hydralisks to bring along. If you choose to go this route, be sure that the first row of Missile Turrets has been destroyed before you try to drop your troops on enemy ground. This takes careful timing because of the slow movement of the Overlords, but if you want a ground war, you'll have to transport your troops over.

Resource Management

The limiting factor in this scenario is Vespene Gas. You'll most likely have to capture the central island to get the 5,000 Vespene Gas units awaiting your harvest. Once the extra Vespene is flowing in, you should be able to manufacture the double-pronged attack most effective for capturing the Command Center.

To make the suggested air assault, you must build a Spire and upgrade it to a Greater Spire. You'll also need to build up your Hatchery to Hive status, and research your Overlords' transport ability. By the end of the mission you'll probably find you've researched the entire available tech tree, anyway.

Fig. 5-10:

Map of Zerg Mission 4.

Mission Overview

While Daggoth is occupied with Dominion forces, emanations from the Chrysalis lure more enemy forces. The Overmind informs you that, although you can destroy these enemy forces, your primary objective remains protecting the Chrysalis as it nears the time of hatching.

Mission Objectives

* Protect the Chrysalis until it's ready to hatch.
* Infest or destroy Raynor's Command Center.
* Kerrigan must survive.

Special Units

* Chrysalis
* Kerrigan (Zerg)
* Jim Raynor (enemy)

New Units

* Infested Terran
* Queen

Battle Strategy

Build up a solid defense matrix of Sunken Colonies and Spore Colonies around your base as soon as possible. The Terrans will regularly drop in small groups of Marines and Firebats, and although the Hydralisks and Zerglings you start with will provide some defense, you'll need backup.

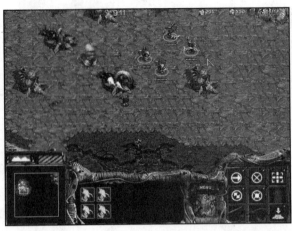

Fig. 5-11:
The Terrans will drop continually to attack your base, so protect it well.

After you secure your main base, you should create a modest group of Mutalisks to fly over and secure the air space over the central island. You probably won't meet any resistance at first, but as you begin to build a Hatchery the Terrans will begin to airlift in plenty of units to hinder your progress. You should take enough Mutalisks to defend the island until you can build up some Spore Colonies and Sunken Colonies for defense. An Overlord must drop in at least one Drone in order to start a new Hatchery, so be sure to protect the Overlord as it lumbers over to the island.

TIP

Use Kerrigan

Have Kerrigan help secure the central island if you're having trouble with the Terran troops dropping in. She's very powerful and can do substantial damage to the enemy.

Vast Terran forces lie in all corners of the map except the upper left (where you started), but you needn't battle them all. Don't pick fights; just stay cool and establish your base on the Central Island. Once this base is up and running, continue to build a force of Mutalisks to act as your primary strike force against the Terran Command Center. Two full groups of Mutalisks should be more than enough. Because the Command Center can't be reached by land, the air attack is a prudent strategy. You can also take a Queen along to infest the Command Center, if destroying it doesn't appeal to you.

MISSION #4:
Agent of the Swarm

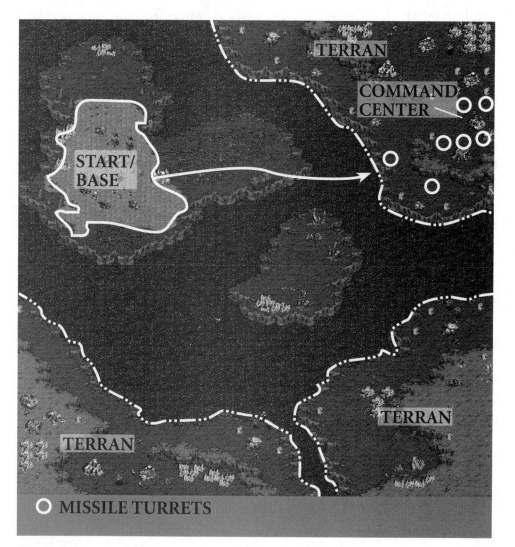

Fig. 5-10:
Map of Zerg Mission 4.

Mission Overview

While Daggoth is occupied with Dominion forces, emanations from the Chrysalis lure more enemy forces. The Overmind informs you that, although you can destroy these enemy forces, your primary objective remains protecting the Chrysalis as it nears the time of hatching.

Mission Objectives

* Protect the Chrysalis until it's ready to hatch.
* Infest or destroy Raynor's Command Center.
* Kerrigan must survive.

Special Units

* Chrysalis
* Kerrigan (Zerg)
* Jim Raynor (enemy)

New Units

* Infested Terran
* Queen

Battle Strategy

Build up a solid defense matrix of Sunken Colonies and Spore Colonies around your base as soon as possible. The Terrans will regularly drop in small groups of Marines and Firebats, and although the Hydralisks and Zerglings you start with will provide some defense, you'll need backup.

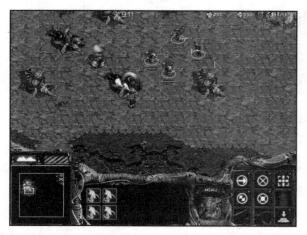

Fig. 5-11:

The Terrans will drop continually to attack your base, so protect it well.

After you secure your main base, you should create a modest group of Mutalisks to fly over and secure the air space over the central island. You probably won't meet any resistance at first, but as you begin to build a Hatchery the Terrans will begin to airlift in plenty of units to hinder your progress. You should take enough Mutalisks to defend the island until you can build up some Spore Colonies and Sunken Colonies for defense. An Overlord must drop in at least one Drone in order to start a new Hatchery, so be sure to protect the Overlord as it lumbers over to the island.

TIP

Use Kerrigan

Have Kerrigan help secure the central island if you're having trouble with the Terran troops dropping in. She's very powerful and can do substantial damage to the enemy.

Vast Terran forces lie in all corners of the map except the upper left (where you started), but you needn't battle them all. Don't pick fights; just stay cool and establish your base on the Central Island. Once this base is up and running, continue to build a force of Mutalisks to act as your primary strike force against the Terran Command Center. Two full groups of Mutalisks should be more than enough. Because the Command Center can't be reached by land, the air attack is a prudent strategy. You can also take a Queen along to infest the Command Center, if destroying it doesn't appeal to you.

Fig. 5-12:

Use a strong force of Mutalisks to neutralize the Terran Missile Turrets before you attempt a ground-unit landing.

When you first begin your aerial assault, bring your ships in two waves, with the first wave taking the Missile Turrets quickly, and then the second wave to attack miscellaneous ground units, such as Marines and Goliaths. Mutalisks are good for these kinds of targets because their attacks bounce from one enemy unit to another, inflicting collateral damage on adjacent units. After the Missile Turrets have been destroyed, you can bring in your Queen and infest the Command Center to win the mission.

If you don't like the idea of an all-out air attack, you'll need to research Overlord Transport and pack up some Zerglings and Hydralisks to bring along. If you choose to go this route, be sure that the first row of Missile Turrets has been destroyed before you try to drop your troops on enemy ground. This takes careful timing because of the slow movement of the Overlords, but if you want a ground war, you'll have to transport your troops over.

Resource Management

The limiting factor in this scenario is Vespene Gas. You'll most likely have to capture the central island to get the 5,000 Vespene Gas units awaiting your harvest. Once the extra Vespene is flowing in, you should be able to manufacture the double-pronged attack most effective for capturing the Command Center.

To make the suggested air assault, you must build a Spire and upgrade it to a Greater Spire. You'll also need to build up your Hatchery to Hive status, and research your Overlords' transport ability. By the end of the mission you'll probably find you've researched the entire available tech tree, anyway.

MISSION #5:
THE AMERIGO

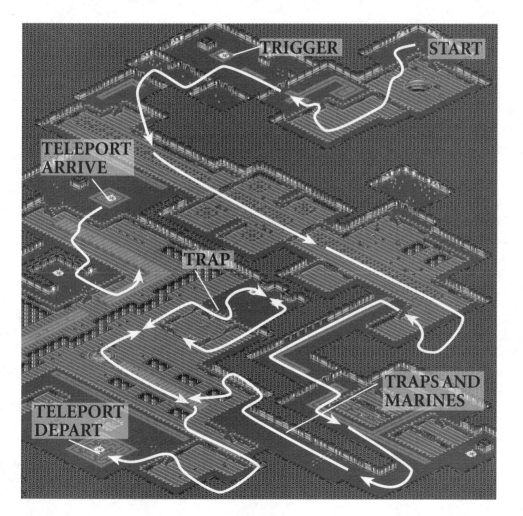

Fig. 5-13:

Map of Zerg Mission 5.

Mission Overview

Now that the Chrysalis has hatched and Kerrigan has become an instrument of the Zerg, she's eager to explore the full scope of her psionic powers. The Terrans limit the psionic abilities of Ghosts so their powers can't be used against the Confederacy, but now that Kerrigan is a Zerg she wants to reach her full potential. You must protect her at all costs as she searches for the Supercomputer that will provide the information she needs.

Mission Objectives

  ✴ Take Kerrigan to the Supercomputer.
  ✴ Kerrigan must survive.

Special Unit

  ✴ Kerrigan
  ✴ Hunter Killers

New Enemy Units (Terran)

  ✴ N/A

Battle Strategy

This mission offers you only the units on the map. Although you can get reinforcements later on, you can't manufacture new units

The Amerigo is a technological maze, so it would be pointless to describe how to wind through to the Supercomputer. Instead, refer to figure 5-13 for a route through the installation. The only proviso is that there's a teleport pad that takes you directly to the Supercomputer area once you've wound through much of the base. You also must walk onto all Beacons to unlock all the doors.

As you negotiate the corridors you'll encounter Marines, Firebats, Ghosts, and Vultures, but usually not more than four at a time. Your ace in the hole is Kerrigan, whose 400 hit points, Cloak, and powerful attack give you the edge you need. Whenever things get hot, have Kerrigan move in to kick some butt.

 CAUTION There's a trap for your troops (see map) where all the doors close around you and there are floor mounted guns that can see Kerrigan even when cloaked. You can fight your way through this by keeping out of range of the floor-mounted guns and just picking off the Marines, then taking the F-M guns out.

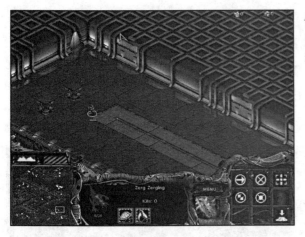

Fig. 5-14:

Watch out for these floor-mounted guns.

Fig. 5-15:

You must use these teleport pads to reach the Supercomputer.

Kerrigan's cloaking also can help you scout areas where you suspect there may be wall-mounted guns or enemy units. In fact, using Kerrigan as a scout who can walk past and flank enemy troops while your Hydralisks mount a frontal attack can work very well.

Resource Management

There's no resource management for this mission. However, if you get low on units, a closed room holds a pack of Zerglings eager to help if only you'll pick them up.

MISSION #6:
THE DARK TEMPLAR

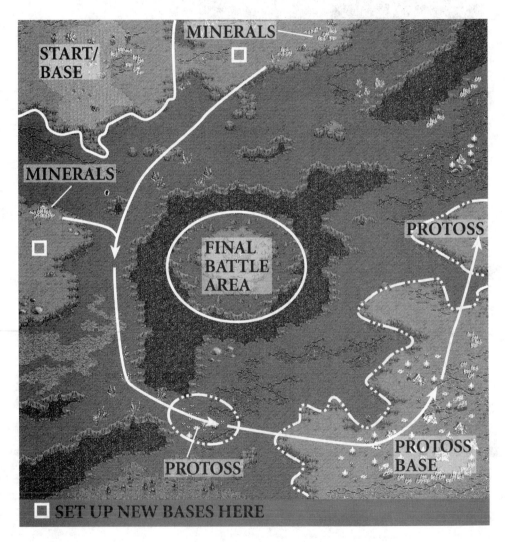

START/
BASE

MINERALS

MINERALS

FINAL
BATTLE
AREA

PROTOSS

PROTOSS

PROTOSS
BASE

☐ SET UP NEW BASES HERE

Fig. 5-16:

Map of Zerg Mission 6.

Mission Overview

Kerrigan senses that the Protoss are hidden on Char. She's declared herself Queen of the Zerg and challenges the Protoss commander, Tassadar of the Templar, to a battle to the death. The Templar voices his disappointment that Kerrigan, once a proud fighter for the Terran cause, has fallen to the Overmind. Kerrigan, however, is happy where she is and will stop at nothing to see the Templar and his forces destroyed.

Mission Objectives

* Exterminate the Protoss intruders.
* Kerrigan must survive.
* Take Kerrigan to meet Tassadar, alone.
* Defeat the Templar.

Special Units

* Kerrigan
* Tassadar (Protoss Templar)

New Unit

* Guardians

New Enemy Unit (Protoss)

* Reavers

Battle Strategy

The Protoss attack regularly with Zealots, Dragoons, and, later on, Scouts. Don't go looking for trouble by wandering toward the lower-right corner of the map or you'll have reams of Dragoons flowing up to your main base. Branch out to the resource areas in the upper-middle and left-middle map areas, and try to set up defenses for these areas, as well.

Fig. 5-17:

Build up defenses because you'll see plenty of Dragoons in the early part of this mission.

It won't be easy to handle the Protoss onslaught up the left side of the map, but if you can build up a solid base of Hydralisks you can defend yourself adequately until you can do the research you need to get Guardians. Hydralisks are relatively cheap, and they're excellent against both ground and air units. They're not completely effective against the powerful Protoss units, however, so always attack and defend in numbers.

Fig. 5-18:

This three-pronged strike force is just the ticket.

Your strike force in this mission should be three groups of ground and air units. You'll need to have eight to ten Mutalisks, and convert eight to ten additional Mutalisks to Guardians. For the ground units, the Hydralisk is unsurpassed. This combination gives the Guardians the raw bombing power they need to take out a Photon Cannon in two volleys, while the Mutalisks can deal with Scouts that may come to take out the Guardians. The Hydralisks serve three purposes: They can attack stray ground units, back up your Guardians by attacking air units, and effectively level buildings on their own.

Move down the left side of the map, across the bottom, and up the right side. This combined air/ground force should be able to take out the entire Protoss installation, but it's not easy, and you may end up losing your attack force. Therefore, you should have a smaller backup force under construction as you make your initial attack run.

Fig. 5-19:

Use your special powers to defeat the Templar in the showdown at the end of the mission.

After you've taken out enough structures, Tassadar challenges Kerrigan to a duel in the central map area. Have an Overlord transport Kerrigan over (it's only accessible from the air), and make sure that she isn't near death. When Kerrigan arrives, Tassadar appears and exchanges a few words with Kerrigan, then disappears and the level is over. You win.

Resource Management

Your goal for this mission is to capture (and hold) the two resource areas in the upper-middle and left-middle map areas. After setting up a few Spore Colonies and Sunken Colonies to defend your starting position, branch out to take the new resource areas. Speed is important in this scenario: The Protoss continue attacking in waves as the scenario progresses, and the more time you spend defending against their attacks, the fewer resources will be left for you to mount an attack with.

MISSION #7:
THE CULLING

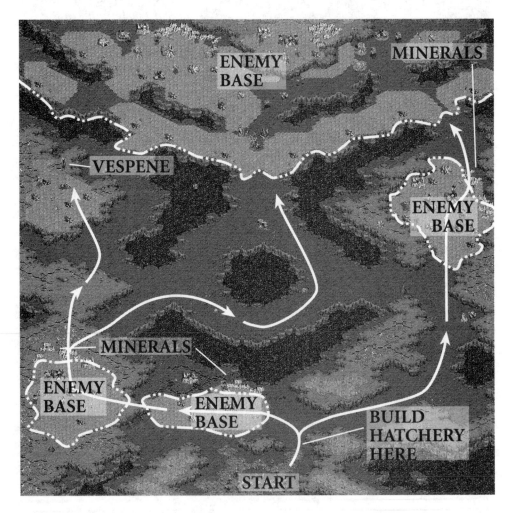

Fig. 5-20:

Map of Zerg Mission 7.

Mission Overview

Kerrigan is chastised for her aggressive stance against Tassadar because during her fight with the Templar, the Cerebrate Zasz was killed. The Protoss have found an attack powerful enough to nullify the Cerebrates' reincarnation ability, leaving the Garm Brood rampaging toward the Central Hive. You must eradicate every last member of the now-leaderless Garm Brood.

Mission Objectives

* Eradicate every last remnant of the Garm Brood.
* Kerrigan must survive.

Special Unit

* N/A

New Unit

* Defiler

New Enemy Units (Zerg)

* Ultralisk

Battle Strategy

This mission can be tough. Get too aggressive right off the bat, and you're guaranteed to get smoked by enemy Zerg.

You begin with a sizable force sitting in an area the enemy surrounds. There are two paths out of the canyon where you start out, but again, you shouldn't move any units out until after you establish a Hatchery and a Sunken Colony for defense. Set up your new Hatchery at the mouth of the pathway to the right; then build a Creep Colony (followed by a Sunken Colony) as soon as the Creep is established.

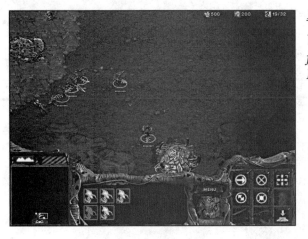

**Fig. 5-21:**

You'll have to sneak around at first to establish your Hatchery.

Group your Hydralisks and Mutalisks separately. After the Hatchery and Sunken Colony are in place, move your attack force up to the enemy Hatchery just to the north of your starting position. The enemy Creep is lightly defended and you shouldn't have too much trouble clearing out the Garm Brood Hydralisks, Zerglings and buildings. As you clear away the enemy base, move your Drones up to build another Hatchery closer to the Vespene and mineral sources.

 You begin with only a finite number of resources and no initial base, so be careful that you don't get into a situation where you lose your Drones. If you lose your Drones before you have established a Hatchery, the game is over.

As you build up your base, be sure to build Spore Colonies and Sunken Colonies to defend against stray attackers. After you establish your base and take the mineral fields in the lower-left map area, build up two groups of 12 Zerglings each. Take these Zergling groups and follow the path (see figure 5-20) to the enemy installations. Don't let anything panic you! Send your Zergling groups in to attack anything and everything. You'll overwhelm the enemy with these vicious little creatures and sweep through a large portion of the enemy infrastructure before they're wiped out.

TIP

Use the Queen

Zerg Queens have a unique ability to infest enemy units with a parasite enabling you to see through the enemy's eyes. Infecting a few patrolling enemy Overlords can provide you with intelligence that will help you plan your attacks.

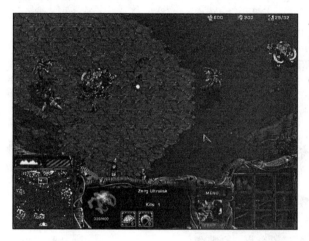

Fig. 5-22:

The Ultralisk can be scary, but if you attack in force, taking it out is manageable.

Now that the enemy's back on its heels, you can take time to build up a solid strike force of Guardians and Hydralisks to finish the job. Keep going until you've wiped out every last structure, but be wary of Ultralisks awaiting you at the top of the map. These are very powerful and will cut through Zerglings quickly, so keep Hydralisks and/or Guardians nearby when moving into enemy territory.

Resource Management

You have only a modest pool of resources to work with in the beginning, so it's critical that you can establish a Hatchery and get new minerals coming in before roving bands of enemy Hydralisks kill your Drones. Set up your Hatchery just above the narrow area off the right-hand path leading out of the canyon you start in. After the Hatchery is up, build a Creep Colony and Spawning Pool; then convert the Creep Colony into a Sunken Colony.

As soon as you're engaged in battle around the enemy Hatchery, you can send your remaining Drones over to sneak minerals back to your own Hatchery. Once the enemy buildings are destroyed, you can move in and start building your own structures. Eventually, with the help of Kerrigan's Psionic Storm, you can stem the tide of enemy units coming in to retake the area and can build another Hatchery closer to the mineral field. Next, concentrate on building up requisite structures and researching technologies you'll need later on. You'll have access to Defilers in this scenario, although it probably will take you awhile to get them. To use them in your attacks, hold off on the Zergling sweep until after you research Defiler technology.

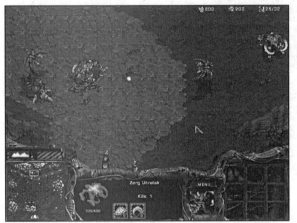

Fig. 5-22:

A group of Hydralisks can do a surprising amount of damage. Keep an extra group of 12 handy in case your main attack force needs backup.

MISSION #8:
EYE FOR AN EYE

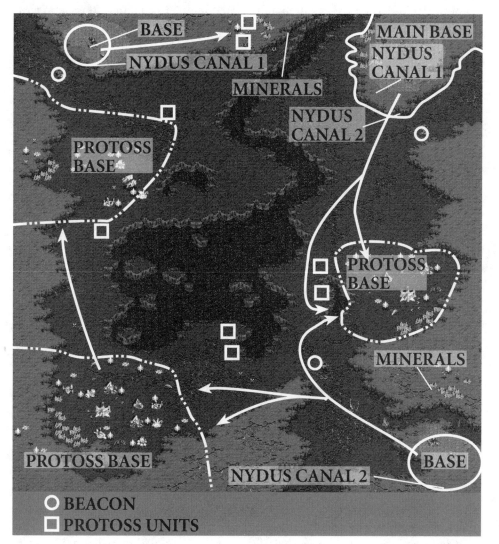

Fig. 5-24:
Map of Zerg Mission 8.

Mission Overview

The Overmind is disturbed because the Dark Templar can radiate energies that are much like its own. These energies enabled the Protoss to murder the Cerebrate Zasz, and have harmed the Overmind. But when Zeratul murdered Zasz, his mind contacted the Overlord's, and all the Protoss secrets became available to the Zerg consciousness. Now the Zerg know where to find the location of Aiur, the Protoss homeworld, but you must ensure that the Dark Templars inflict no more damage on the Zerg.

Mission Objectives

* Destroy the Protoss base.
* Let no Dark Templar escape.
* Kerrigan must survive.

Special Units

* Infested Kerrigan
* Dark Templar (Protoss)

New Units

* Nydus Canal
* Ultralisk

New Enemy Units (Protoss)

* Archon
* High Templar

Battle Strategy

Once you've got a solid force of Drones collecting resources, build up a defensive force of Hydralisks to keep an eye on your bases and Beacons. If even one Dark Templar slips by the Beacon areas, you'll lose, so it pays to keep a few extra units handy. You can divide the units among the three locations or use the Nydus Canal to send them to attack the sources. The enemy will constantly test the Beacon sites, and even attack your bases on occasion, so your Hydralisk support forces will serve you well.

TIP The Nydus Canals are handy little structures that enable your forces essentially to teleport from one area to another almost instantly. The Nydus Canals can get units to hot spots in a few seconds, and since Zerg Mission #8 has a Nydus Canal network already in place, you can use it as a defense transport between your bases.

Fig. 5-25:

Get a decent group of Hydralisks in place at each Beacon until you can establish a new base.

Build up a force of 10 to 12 Hydralisks by your base in the upper left corner of the map; then move toward the resource area in the upper-middle area of the map. You'll encounter some Protoss resistance, but nothing that a group of Hydralisks can't manage. During the fighting consider building a secondary Hydralisk force that can continue to protect the area for a while. (If you've earned the ability to make Mutalisks, you might want to use them for defense instead of the Hydralisks.)

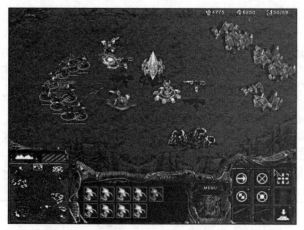

Fig. 5-26:

The resource area in the upper-middle section is only lightly defended, so ten Hydralisks should be able to secure it.

After you've got another base raking in resources in the upper-middle area of the map, sit back (defend) and concentrate on researching missing structures or abilities. Once you feel you're ready, make an air group of eight Guardians and four Mutalisks, a ground group of eight Hydralisks and four Ultralisks, and two single-unit groups with a Queen in one and a Defiler in the other. This will give you the power you need to take out the entire right side of the map so you can secure the resources fields there.

Move your air units up to the edge of the right-hand Protoss base; just close enough to provoke an attack. Once the Protoss come after you, use your ground group to tackle the Dragoons and Zealots while your air group moves in and destroys any Photon Cannons. After the Photon Cannons are gone, the air group can either help with ground units, or pummel the structures into the ground. If a group of Scouts starts to give you trouble, use your Queen to Ensnare them. Likewise, to whittle down an enemy structure or group of units, use the Defiler's Plague ability to leech the life force out of the targeted units. Plagued units usually require only a few hits to destroy.

Fig. 5-27:

These balanced attack forces (along with the Defiler's Dark Swarm and Queen's Ensnare) are all you'll need to take out Protoss bases.

Once the Protoss force is gone, build another Hatchery near the mineral fields and start harvesting the vast resources that line the map's right side. Use these resources to build up another attack force, roughly double in size (to do this right) with a few Zerglings thrown in just for good measure. The Protoss base in the bottom left corner of the map has plenty of Templars standing by, and they won't hesitate to use Psionic Storms to kick your butt.

When you mount the attack on the main Protoss base, take four or five Queens with you to Spawn Broodlings on any Templar they come across. This will help to take care of most of the Templar threat, but you must use Mutalisks to ensure that the body of your attack force doesn't get Psionic deep-fried. After the lower Protoss base falls, the mission is academic. You need only sweep the remaining Protoss off the map to win.

Resource Management

Initially it's important to use the available resources to build up a defense force of Hydralisks at each base and Beacon. Of course it's also important to build all the necessary structures and research the entire tech tree, but before you can progress comfortably you'll need to have at least four Hydralisks at each Beacon.

Once you're secure in your positions you'll need more resources to wipe out the Protoss bases, so set up a new base in the upper-middle portion of the map (you'll need to clear this area of Protoss first). There's another resource area just above your base in the lower-right corner of the map, although you'll need to airlift your Drones to that area if you don't want to fight through a Protoss base en route.

Build up your tech tree to where you can use the Defiler's and Queen's special abilities during your attacks. These technological extras come in handy against the Protoss.

MISSION #9:
The Invasion of Aiur

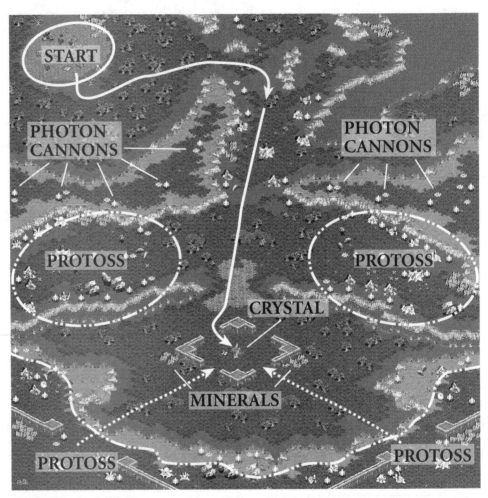

Fig. 5-28:

Map of Zerg Mission 9.

Mission Overview

The Overmind is certain victory is at hand: On the world of Aiur, the Zerg will bring the strongest known creature into the Zerg fold. However, before it can incorporate this new species into the swarm, you must prepare the way. You must seize the Khaydarin Crystals to secure a power greater than any the Protoss have ever known.

Mission Objectives

* Take a Drone to the Khaydarin Crystal Formation.

Special Structure

* Khaydarin Crystal

New Unit

* N/A

New Enemy Units (Protoss)

* Arbiter
* Carrier

Battle Strategy

There are enough high-end Protoss units in this scenario to pound you into the stone age, so don't attempt a war of attrition. However, that doesn't mean you won't get your hands dirty. Indeed, there's plenty of fighting ahead.

The Khaydarin Crystal sits just below the center of the map; many Protoss units literally surround it. Setting up some defenses (Sunken Colonies and Spore Colonies) is critically important to protecting your base, although you shouldn't pour tons of resources into a massive defense matrix. Stay in defense mode until you can create Hydralisks, Zerglings, Queens, Scourges, and Overlord Transports.

Try to be quick about this mission. The longer you wait to build up your forces, the greater the chance the enemy will show up with a bunch of Dragoons and a Carrier or two to ruin your day. Build up a force of full groups of Zerglings (2 full groups), Hydralisks, and Scourge. The Zerglings and Hydralisks are cheap, but in force they can ensure success in your push through the canyons to the Crystal.

Fig. 5-29:

Getting a Drone to this Crystal is your goal.

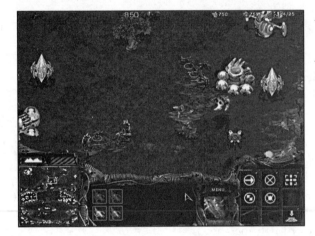

Fig. 5-30:

This swarming group of Zerglings can do more damage to the mighty Protoss than you might think.

Follow the path shown in figure 5-28 and use your Zerglings as the first-wave attackers, with the Hydralisks close behind. The Zerglings are so plentiful (24, at least) that the Protoss units and Photon Cannons will have difficulty zeroing in on any one target, leaving the door open for your more powerful Hydralisks to do the real damage. The Scourge are basically Carrier killers, in case one comes after your units. If you do see a Carrier on the horizon, send all the Scourge at it at once. Don't hesitate for a second, because a Carrier can decimate your force very quickly.

Counterpoint

NOTE

If you take too long to mount your offense and you find yourself falling into defensive mode just to keep the Protoss out of your base, you'll end up in a resource drain. This isn't the end of the world; you just have to move on to Plan B. There are three resource areas in the north portion of the map. All are lightly defended by the Protoss, but not colonized. The problem is you must find a way to get a Drone to one of these areas alive. The upper-right map corner has two of the best areas (two mineral fields and one Vespene Geyser), and they aren't directly defended. If you can get a unit to this area, build a Hatchery, and then a Nydus Canal, you can double your resources quickly. From this resource base you'll have a fighting chance to hit back at the Protoss forces.

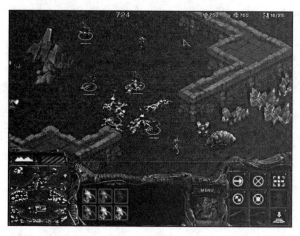

Fig. 5-31:

After you get a Drone into the Khaydarin Crystal, you must defend the area from Protoss assaults until the Crystal can be extracted.

   Once the pathway to the Crystal is clear, you can either move a Drone down (via the ground) or you can transport it with an Overlord. Both routes can be risky, but if you use an Overlord you must be careful to follow the path you cleared. If you go as the crow flies, your Overlord will get toasted by the array of Photon Cannons lining the ridge between you and the Crystal.
   When the Drone enters the Crystal, it triggers a 10 minute countdown as well as a Protoss attack. You'll need to continue to move units down to the Crystal in order to hold the location while the Crystal is being harvested. Enemy units that are particularly devastating at this point include Templars, Carriers, and especially Reavers. The Reavers can take out a row of Hydralisks with just one or two Scarabs, so stay cool and use Guardian Air support if you can. If you successfully hold the Crystal for 10 minutes, you will win the mission. Don't go picking any fights either, the Protoss forces in the lower left and right corners of the map don't need to be awakened.

Resource Management

Again, there are two ways to approach this mission:

1. Build up a relatively cheap, large strike force to go in and clear a path to the Crystal before the enemy has a chance to accumulate an arsenal.

2. Plan for a long, involved conflict wiping the Protoss off half the map, and secure the untapped resource centers in the map's northeast corner.

Either way is acceptable; indeed, the first strategy often bleeds into the second (literally) when the Protoss offer up a little too much resistance and drain your resources.

Before you get into high-end technology development, use your resources to create a large and cheap strike force. This way you can give it a try; if you fail, you can fall back on getting superior units. To create the strike force you'll need, it's handy to have a second Hatchery going, so build one if you can afford it.

MISSION #10:
FULL CIRCLE

Fig. 5-32:

Map of Zerg Mission 10.

Mission Overview

The Protoss can do nothing but flee before the Zerg Swarm, but you must assault one final site to guarantee your conquest. You must clear the temple that stands on hallowed Protoss ground to set the Khaydarin Crystal in its place. Once you complete this task, the Overmind will manifest.

Mission Objective

✳ Destroy the Protoss temple.

Fig. 5-33:

Get your base up and running quickly to exploit fully the vast mineral supplies nearby.

Battle Strategy

Build and conquer—that's the name of the game in this scenario. Once you've produced a pile of Drones and two new Hatcheries to maximize harvesting and unit production, build Sunken Colonies and Spore Colonies galore around the perimeter of your base. It's also a good idea to have a team of 12 Hydralisks ready in case of Protoss attack.

After fending off Protoss attacks and climbing the tech tree until you have Guardians and upgraded Hydralisks, build a force of eight Guardians and four Mutalisks (one group), 12 Hydralisks (one group), 12 Hydralisks (one group), and mixed units (one group). Hotkey these units to keys **1-4**, and move them up the map toward the temple (follow the path in figure 5-32). Destroy any Photon Cannons or offensive Protoss units you come across. The Guardians can take out Protoss structures quickly, so sweep a clean path for your Drone to follow with the Crystal.

En route to the Temple you'll face some stiff opposition from Photon Cannons and ground forces (Zealots and Dragoons), and a Carrier awaits you at the temple. Target it first to eliminate that threat. When the enemy presence at the temple is almost gone, hit it with your Guardians while your Hydralisks mop up Zealots and nearby structures. When the Crystal Drone appears, grab an Overlord and transport the Drone to the Beacon near the temple rubble.

Fig. 5-34:

Attacking in force like this will overwhelm the Protoss forces.

Fig. 5-35:

After you take out the temple you need only get the Drone that's carrying the Crystal to the Beacon.

Resource Management

You won't want for minerals in this scenario, but you'll need an air force to win decisively, so you'll need gas—and that's not as plentiful. However, mount your attacks effectively and you can destroy the temple without securing new mineral or gas locations.

You have a vast supply of minerals at your disposal right away, so produce lots of Drones to engage in a frenzied harvest of minerals and gas. Set up plenty of Spore Colonies and Sunken Colonies to protect your base. Otherwise, just concentrate on climbing the tech tree until you can create Guardians and your Hydralisks have maximum benefits. If you need more resource areas, the one in the map's lower-left corner is most vulnerable.

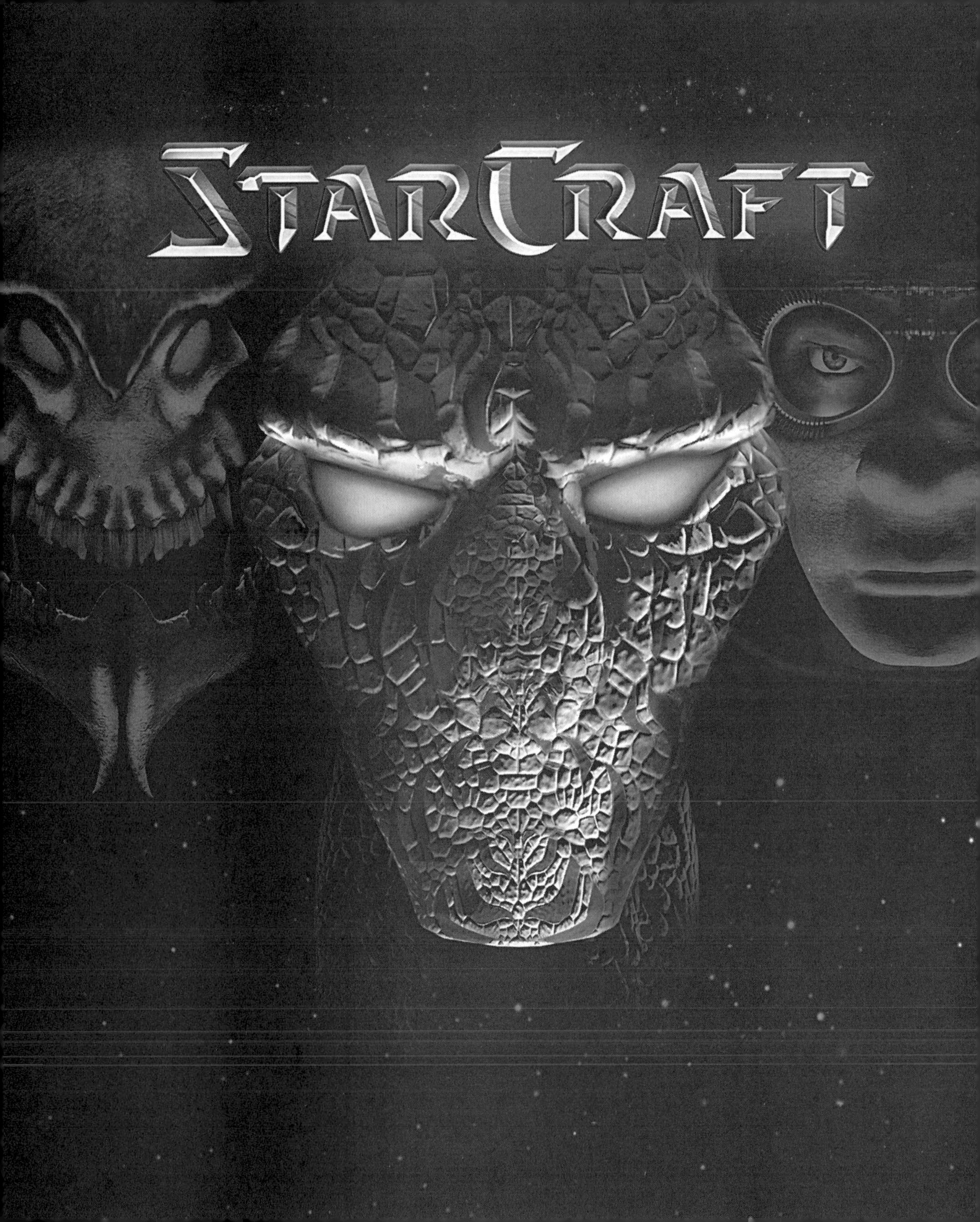
StarCraft

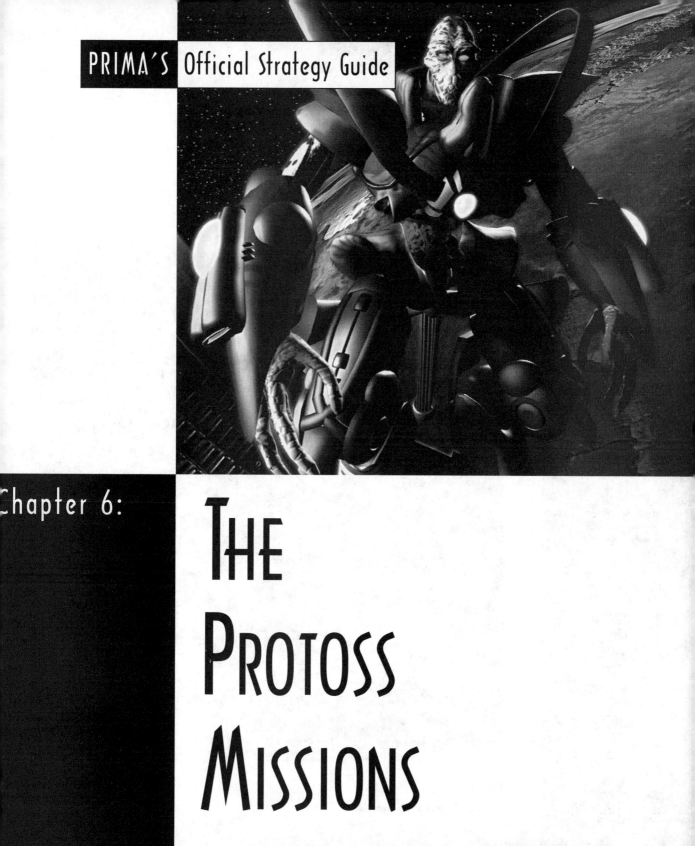

Chapter 6:

THE PROTOSS MISSIONS

MISSION #1:
First Strike

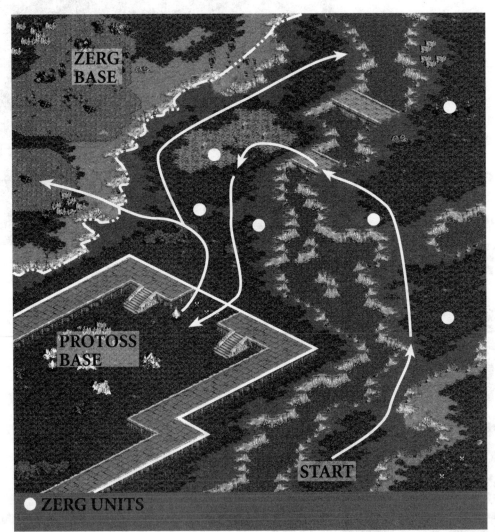

ZERG BASE

PROTOSS BASE

START

● ZERG UNITS

Fig. 6-1:

Map of Protoss Mission 1.

Mission Overview

The Conclave has sent Judicator Aldaris to counsel you: The former Executor, Tassadar, disregarded orders and attempted to destroy the Zerg while sparing the Terrans from the flame. The Conclave dictates that the first priority is strengthening defenses. You must reinforce and defend the outpost at Antioch.

Mission Objectives

* Meet Fenix at Antioch.
* Destroy the Zerg base.
* Fenix must survive.

Special Units

* Fenix

New Units

* Zealot
* Dragoon

Battle Strategy

This mission starts in the lower-right corner of the map. You must move your units up and around the body of water and through a couple of Zerg patrols to get to the base at Antioch. Once there, you can liberate all the units simultaneously by capturing the Nexus. As you set up your base to produce more units for your attack, it's a good idea take all your offensive units (except two Zealots) and group them into an attack squad.

Take the attack squad up into the main Zerg base and wreak some havoc. Beware: Where there appear to be no Zerg, there often are. Many Zerg units on this map are buried, so keep an eye on your attack squad as they move across the map. When you run into Sunken Colonies and Hydralisks, move your Zealots in aggressively and take out as much as you initially can. This quick attack sets the Zerg back on their heels and gives you time to build structures to create the group of Dragoons you'll use to clear the skies of the Mutalisk menace.

When you have a solid finishing force—six Zealots and six Dragoons will do nicely—you can sweep the rest of the map and take out the remaining Zerg infestation.

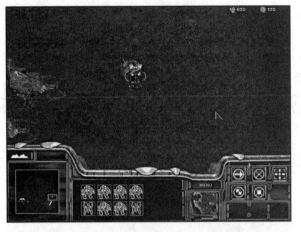

<u>*Fig. 6-02:*</u>

You'll run into a couple of Zerg patrols en route to Antioch.

<u>*Fig. 6-3:*</u>

Eventually you'll need to create more Dragoons to deal with the Mutalisks roaming the map.

Resource Management

This is the first Protoss mission, so take your time and get used to Protoss conventions. Specifically, Pylons equate to Supply Depots (Terran) and Overlords (Zerg), and you can build new structures only within a specified radius of one of these structures. Once a Probe opens a warp rift, the rift will continue to open by itself, leaving the probe free to perform other tasks.

You're given a substantial enough force in this first mission that you needn't sweat the resource gathering/building process. Instead, take your time and learn the nuances of the Protoss technologies (as much as you can at this point) as you build up your structures. Note that the Protoss units are comparatively expensive, so you'll need a larger fleet of Probes to finance a large army.

MISSION #2:
INTO THE FLAMES

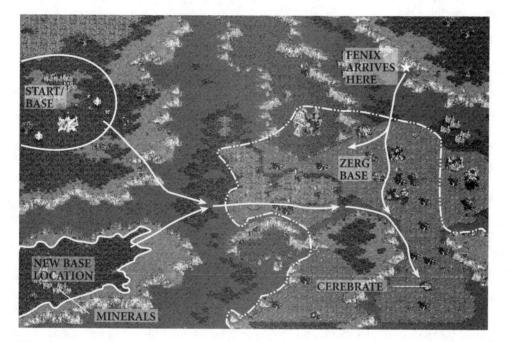

Fig. 6-4:

Map of Protoss Mission 2.

Mission Overview

Your defense of Antioch has restored Aldaris's faith in the Templar castle. Tassadar, who has been missing for some time, contacts Aldaris and admits he's had contact with the Fallen Ones—the Dark Templar. Tassadar has learned that the Zerg's strength lies in their unity, and that the Overmind's control over the Zerg is dispensed through underlings called Cerebrates. If you can destroy the Cerebrates, perhaps you can exterminate the Zerg.

Mission Objectives

* Distract the Zerg while Fenix gets into position.
* Kill the Zerg Cerebrate.
* Fenix must survive.

Special Units

* Fenix (Protoss)
* Cerebrate (Zerg)

New Units

* N/A

Battle Strategy

First, you'll need to place your existing offensive units near the ramp leading up to the platform where your base sits. The Zerg will launch attack after attack on this position, as well as an attack or two from the plains north of your base. As with the last mission, plenty of Zerg units lie in wait underground, so remember that nothing is as it seems.

As soon as your resource pool is rising, build a pair of Photon Cannons at the top of the ramp. This will save you huge amounts of trouble later. Photon Cannons are particularly handy because they can engage both land and air targets equally. Build up an army of Zealots and Dragoons and just sit tight until the requisite 15 minutes have passed.

Fig. 6-05:

Set up several Photon Cannons to protect your base from the swarming Zerg.

Fig. 6-6:

Setting up a new Nexus by the mineral field in the lower right corner of the map is important to your victory.

After 15 minutes, Fenix and his group of units will appear in the upper-right map corner. Distract the Zerg forces with careful but annoying (for the Zerg) attacks against their base, just below Fenix's troops. At the same time, move your attack force out of your base and head toward the lower-right map corner, where the Cerebrate awaits his death. There are plenty of Sunken Colonies and buried Hydralisks and Zerglings en route to the Cerebrate, so pay close attention; above all, *keep moving forward*. After you reach the Cerebrate, five or six Zealots can kill it in fairly short order. Consider using a pincer attack, with your two forces meeting up just before the final push toward the Cerebrate, but take care to keep Fenix alive or the mission will fail.

Resource Management

The area around the base has all the resources you need to develop a solid force to take out the Cerebrate. Once your defenses are set up (build a few Photon Cannons around the base), concentrate on gathering as many resources as possible: Protoss units are costly. It's important to use Photon Cannons around your base so periodic Zerg attacks don't smoke your expensive Zealots and Dragoons.

MISSION #3:
HIGHER GROUND

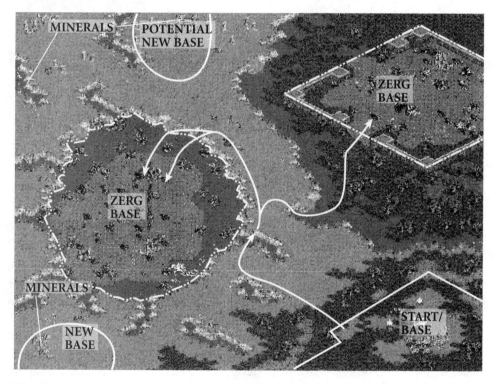

Fig. 6-7:

Map of Protoss Mission 3.

Mission Overview

The Zerg Cerebrate that was thought dead has arisen, and even now drives its brood in preparation for the next Zerg offensive. The conclave is bitter about Tassadar's betrayal, and believes the Protoss can overcome the Zerg only if the conclave focuses all its power. The main strike force will proceed to the province of Psion, while Praetor Fenix stays behind to guard against counterattack.

Mission Objectives

　　✳ Destroy the Zerg colonies.

Special Unit

　　✳ Fenix (Templar)

New Unit

　　✳ Scout

Battle Strategy

This is a good old kill-everything-on-the-map scenario. You begin with your forces nicely established in an enclosed area in the map's lower-right corner. There's only one entrance/exit to this area, and for the first part of the mission this confined area makes for a great defense. The goal is to build up an attack force sufficient to take out both major Zerg populations, but it won't be easy.

First, group your available ground forces (Dragoons and Zealots) into one squad that can react to Zerg attacks. The Zerg consistently will mount attacks against your base, so you must be ready from the start. Build Pylons so you can build Photon Cannons around the perimeter of your base; then build eight or nine Photon Cannons around your base so they will support each other (see figure 6-8). A funnel of six to nine Photon Cannons can turn back the early Zerg attacks, and ultimately will leave you more time and resources to build up your attack force.

Fig. 6-8:

A "funnel" of Photon Cannons will suffice to defend your base in the early going.

After building up a force of eight or so Zealots and a couple of Scouts, move them toward the map's lower-left corner, where you'll find a large resource area. Beware of burrowed Zerg units when you explore this area, and don't just send a Probe to build a Nexus or it will get smoked. Once you've secured the area, have a Nexus in place, and are harvesting resources, take the time to build Pylons and Photon Cannons to defend against an attack from down on the left side of the map. Once the Zerg know you're establishing a new base, they'll mass forces along there for a counterattack.

Fig. 6-9:

Defend any new bases you establish, because the enemy will eagerly come after these weak positions.

After setting up your second base, continue building up your forces as you research what remains in the tech tree. Although it may be possible to take one very large force and wipe out the entire Zerg presence, it's not easy (and not recommended). It's much easier to take the two main Zerg bases out one at a time with substantial attack forces.

Build up at least 12 Zealots (preferably 20), eight Scouts, and ten Dragoons; then move up the middle of the map to take out the base on the left. With the Scouts providing air cover, move your attack force into the left-hand Zerg base and attack aggressively. It won't be pretty, and you can expect to lose about half your units. As this battle rages, the other Zerg base ferries units over to help out, but your Scouts should be able to catch them before they disrupt your attacking forces.

Fig. 6-10:

Once you destroy the left-hand Zerg Base, you'll be well on your way to victory.

After you destroy the left-hand Zerg base, build a Nexus and harvest any remaining minerals and gases. For that matter, you can move north safely to an area where there are even more mineral fields. Having destroyed half the Zerg, you can sit back and rebuild your attack force, this time making it a little larger. When everything is in place, mount an attack on the right-hand Zerg base. If it falters, it should be very easy (in terms of resources) to get a mop-up force in place quickly.

Resource Management

Immediately use the 300 minerals you start with to build six new Probes; set them all to harvest minerals. Continue this process until the money starts building up. Once you have some extra cash and have placed the extra Pylons and Photon Cannons near the gate, begin building up your technologies. In this scenario it helps a great deal if you can follow the tech tree as far as you can: Given the Zerg's overwhelming numbers, weapons are important to your forces.

There's a large mineral and Vespene field in the map's lower-left corner. Although you can win without making a new base in this area, building a Nexus there and harvesting those resources is a very good idea. In the end, having the extra resource pool makes your job a lot easier.

MISSION #4:
THE HUNT FOR TASSADAR

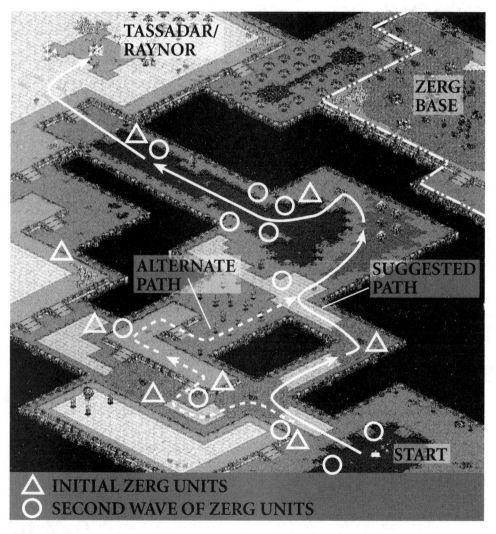

Fig. 6-11:

Map of Protoss Mission 4.

Mission Overview

You were reluctant to leave Aiur in its dim hour and you still grieve the loss of Fenix, but your work is not done. Tassadar is now considered the greatest threat to the Protoss race, and you must stop him from spreading the Dark Templar's tainted influence. The Judicator senses a lingering darkness on this world, and you've been summoned to (cautiously) locate the source of the darkness.

Mission Objectives

* Find Tassadar.
* Take Tassadar to the Beacon.
* Take Raynor to the Beacon.

Special Units

* Tassadar (Protoss)
* Jim Raynor (Zerg)

New Units

* High Templar
* Archon

Battle Strategy

You begin this mission in the lower-right corner of the map with a small but potent force of Protoss units. The goal is to find Tassadar, who's at a Protoss base in the upper-left map corner (diagonal to your position). Follow the path on the map in figure 6-11 to find Tassadar, and prepare to face Zerg resistance along the way.

As you work your way toward Tassadar (and the base), try to use your Templar's powers to ease your task. The Psionic Storm (the same as Kerrigan's) can take out entire groups of Hydralisks or Zerglings at once, saving the lives of the units you start with. Once you hack your way up to the base, a dialogue will ensue between the Judicator, Tassadar, and Raynor. At the end, you'll learn you must return both Raynor and Tassadar to the Beacon. That may sound easy, but large numbers of Zerg have appeared—and, in fact, block the path to the Beacon.

Fig. 6-12:

You'll meet moderate Zerg resistance en route to Tassadar's base.

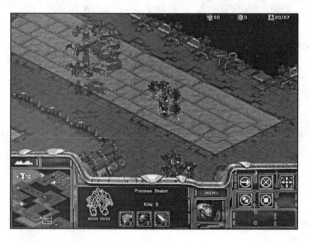

Fig. 6-13:

After you meet Tassadar you must fight your way through another bunch of Zerg to reach the Beacon.

There are a couple of ways to approach the task of getting Tassadar and Raynor back to the Beacon:

1. Take your troops, turn around, and hack your way back to the Beacon.
2. Build up a new army and beat the Zerg back decisively as you make your way to the Beacon.

The first option can be risky, because the Zerg can be overwhelming in numbers and you could lose Raynor or Tassadar. The second option, on the other hand, allows you to climb further up the Protoss tech tree and learn to use the High Templar.

Creating an Archon

Archons are very valuable Protoss units that can only be created from a very special raw material: High Templars. You'll need to have two High Templars to create an Archon—essentially a very powerful unit that can attack both air and ground units. The Archon also has a huge shield protecting it, so a group of Zealots that has a pair of Archons in tow will be formidable. To create an Archon, select two Templars and then click on the Create Archon button in the lower right corner of your screen. It takes a few seconds for the Archon to be summoned, but it's worth the wait.

Fig. 6-14:

There will be some tough battles to fight in order to clear a path back to the Beacon.

When you're ready to make your move toward the Beacon, try to ensure that the units you take can fight units in the air. Several large (and nasty) groups of Hydralisks also wait along the route, so include a pack of Zealots.

Resource Management

This mission gives you a good chance to explore various High Templar abilities. Funnel substantial resources into building up structures and abilities so you can experiment on the Zerg on this level. This mission isn't easy, but you'll still have room to learn about your new Protoss units.

MISSION #5:
CHOOSING SIDES

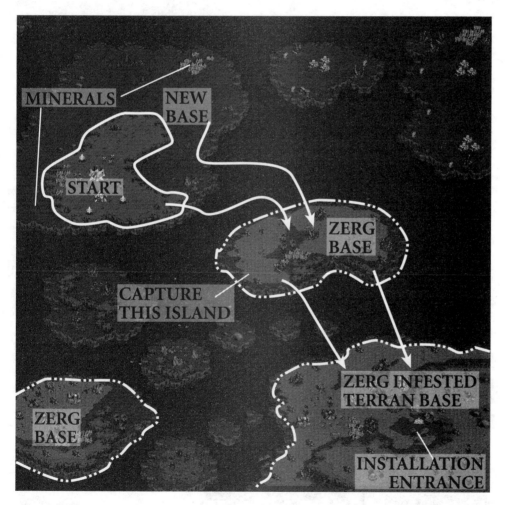

Fig. 6-15:

Map of Protoss Mission 5.

Mission Overview

In following Tassadar and attempting to rescue the Dark Templar, you openly defied the will of the Conclave. The Judicator is disillusioned because he believes that Tassadar is lost to the Protoss. Tassadar learned much from Zeratul, and knows now only the energies of the Dark Templar can truly harm the Zerg. Therefore, to repel the Zerg you must save Zeratul.

Mission Objectives

∗ Bring Tassadar and two Zealots to the installation entrance.

Special Units

∗ Tassadar (Templar)
∗ Raynor (in Vulture)

New Units

∗ Shuttle
∗ Reaver

Battle Strategy

You must take Tassadar and Raynor to the Beacon which lies in the lower-right corner of the map. Your starting point is in the upper-left map corner. The terrain around the six main islands is impassable by land, so mounting an air attack is top priority.

Fig. 6-16:

Setting up near resources should be an early priority.

Take time to build up a substantial base (complete with plenty of Photon Cannons for defense) before venturing into the unknown. Once you have a fleet of six Scouts, take the time to move around the map and define the perimeters of the Zerg bases. The base of greatest interest to you is the island roughly in the center of the map. You need it as a staging area for your assault on the southeast bases.

Fig. 6-17:

The central island is important not only for its resources but also for its strategic location.

When you have six to ten Scouts and three or four loaded Shuttles, move in and attack the central island. Have your Scouts take out air units while your ground troops concentrate on the ground units and Spore Colonies. Be sure to follow up your initial attack with supplementary Shuttles with Dragoons, Zealots, and a couple of Probes. Next, set up a Nexus and begin to build a solid base to launch from.

Fig. 6-18:

The base in the southeast is the best defended, but with a sizable strike force you should be able to gain a foothold.

Continue producing ground units and Scouts as you gather the central island's resources. Many, many Spore Colonies—as well as Guardians, Hydralisks, and Zerglings—defend the southeast island. Therefore it helps if you balance your strike force carefully with Scouts, Zealots, and Dragoons. After assembling the strike force, move in your Scouts first to occupy the Spore Colonies; then quickly move in your Shuttles and drop your Zealots so they can begin the ground war.

Including a strong force of Scouts can make your assault on the sourtheast island much easier than launching a simple ground attack. The Scouts will occupy the enemy Spore Colonies long enough for your Shuttles to get the important fighting troops on the ground. Once the area is secure you can bring in Tassadar and a couple of Zealots in order to satisfy the victory conditions.

Resource Management

Immediately spend your available resources to produce as many Probes as you can afford. Spread out and build a Nexus at every major resource area near your starting location. You may need to develop Shuttles before you can reach some of these areas, but the added resource revenue makes a big difference to how quickly you can amass the troops you need to win.

Once your resource-gathering is in place at multiple locations, build up your technologies until you can manufacture High Templars, Scouts, Shuttles, and Archons. Remember, the Protoss must develop many levels of shields, weapons, and skills if you're to have the most efficient units.

After capturing the central island, build a Nexus and concentrate on harvesting the Vespene; you'll need it to build ships to take out the southern Zerg colony.

MISSION #6:
INTO THE DARKNESS

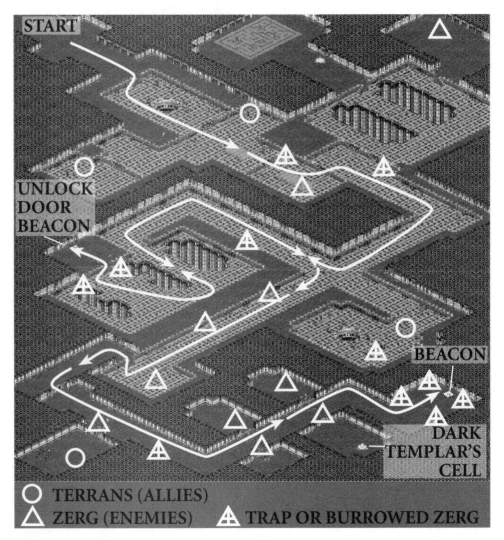

START

UNLOCK
DOOR
BEACON

BEACON

DARK
TEMPLAR'S
CELL

○ TERRANS (ALLIES)
△ ZERG (ENEMIES)
▲ TRAP OR BURROWED ZERG

Fig. 6-19:

Map of Protoss Mission 6.

Mission Overview

Tassadar senses Zeratul and his brethren are close, but he's unable to contact them. Tassadar insists the Protoss scour the area to find the Dark Templar and prevent the Zerg from destroying them. It won't be easy, however, because the Infested Kerrigan is leading the Zerg troops: Her tenacity won't have diminished since her last encounter with Tassadar.

Mission Objectives

* Rescue Zeratul and escort him to the beacon.
* Tassadar and Zeratul must survive.

Special Units

* Tassadar (Templar)
* The Dark Templars

New Enemy Units (Zerg)

* Infested Terran
* Wall-mounted guns
* Floor-mounted guns

Battle Strategy

As you move your Protoss units into the installation, you'll come to a room where Terran Marines have been slaughtered. However, five Marines still stand around waiting for something to happen. Walk up to them to get control of them; you'll need them.

Fig. 6-20:

Not long after you begin this mission you'll come across some Terran Marines. Introduce yourself nicely and they'll give you a hand.

Follow the path through the installation laid out in figure 6-19. Along the way there are plenty of wall-mounted guns, buried Zerglings and Hydralisks, and Infested Terrans. The Infested Terrans pose the biggest threat in this mission, and can take out Tassadar single-handedly, so take care as you walk the halls. Infested Terrans also pop out of secret hiding areas in the floor here, so lead with an expendable Marine or Terran Civilian rather than risk losing Tassadar—and, thus, the scenario.

Fig. 6-21:

Buried Zerglings and Hydralisks abound in this mission, so always lead with expendable units.

As with the other installation missions, you must get to a Beacon to unlock a door that will admit you. As you make your way toward the cell block area you'll face many Zerglings and Infested Terrans, so be sure to liberate teams of Terran Civilians and Marines, Ghosts, and Firebats along the way. These extra units will help get Tassadar to the Beacon.

Fig. 6-22:

Four floor-mounted guns guard the Beacon, so be ready for them.

At the Beacon, four guns pop up out of the floor, taking your forces by surprise. Take them out with whatever you have; if you're low on units the Psionic Storm can do the job. Once you step on the Beacon, the Dark Templar's cell door will open. Take Tassadar into the cell to meet them. It's not easy to see the Templar initially, so don't worry. They'll appear when you walk into the room far enough.

Resource Management

This mission has no resource management component. Note, however, that there are several groups of Terran units that are not your enemies. Whenever you see a group of Terrans, approach them to get them on your side. They'll come in handy later.

MISSION #7:
HOMELAND

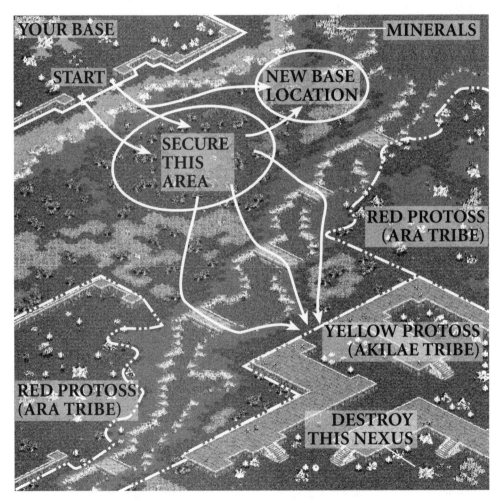

Fig. 6-23:

Map of Protoss Mission 7.

Mission Overview

Although Fenix fell to defeat, the Protoss recovered his ruined body and he lives on within a Dragoon. Fenix tells Tassadar the Aldaris and the Conclave have branded him a traitor and seek to destroy him and Zeratul the Dark Templar. Tassadar and Fenix vow to protect the Dark Templar from the other Protoss. It pains them deeply to do so, but they understand that only by protecting the Dark Templar will they eradicate the Zerg menace.

Mission Objectives

* Destroy the heart of the Conclave.
* Tassadar must survive.
* Fenix must survive.
* Zeratul must survive.

Special Units

* Tassadar (Templar)
* The Dark Templars
* Fenix (in Dragoon)
* Zeratul (Dark Templar)

New Unit

* Observer

New Enemy Unit (Protoss)

* Arbiter

Battle Strategy

Tassadar and the Dark Templar are under attack from Protoss forces. Fall back to your base (in the map's upper-left corner) right away. Don't stay to fight. Enemy forces will follow you back to your base, and your Photon Cannons will take them out before they can break through your line. Then start harvesting minerals and gas posthaste! Use the cash you have in reserve to build up a defensive force of Zealots, Dragoons, and at least three Scouts.

Fig. 6-24:

The enemy will throw plenty of attacks at this position, so stack another couple of Photon Cannons for defense.

Continue building your attack force while you warp in every available structure and research new technologies. Your attack force should comprise at least eight Scouts, 10 Zealots, and 10 Dragoons. You may also want to use some Archons as well, but they are ultimately very expensive. When this attack force is ready, move down the ramp at the front of your base and secure the open area beyond. This area will have enemy units constantly flowing into it, so you must be vigilant in eliminating enemy activity. The enemy probably will throw a couple of larger attacks at you as punishment for expanding, so be ready for that, as well.

Group your Scouts into one large group or two smaller groups. If they are in two smaller groups the two can support each other and it gives you greater protection from Arbiters. Also, enemy Scouts and Arbiters will fall quickly to two large groups of Scouts pounding from two sides. Once you've secured the central area, move a Probe up to the mineral deposits in the map's upper-middle portion and build a Nexus. Start harvesting resources from this area as fast as possible, and continue building units to replace those you'll lose during the skirmishes that follow.

Fig. 6-25:

Wait until you have control over the area beyond your base before attempting to grab this resource area.

When your second base is up and running, move your troops down to the bridges in the map's center. Zerg bases lie on either side, but the one you want is in the lower-right corner. Airlift three or four Reavers (with upgraded Scarabs) in to round out your attack force; then move in for the kill. Have your Reavers target the Photon Cannons (their Scarabs will destroy the Cannons in one shot) while your air group of Scouts moves deep into the base to take out ground units. Your Zealots and Dragoons can follow up and destroy any structures that remain.

When you're pressing to take out the enemy Nexus, expect the other Protoss bases to attack your base with groups of Scouts and be ready for them.

Fig. 6-26:

You can take out the heart of the Conclave with Scouts, but it's easier to match your Scouts up with some ground units, as well.

As you push on toward the Nexus, you'll probably come up against a pair of enemy Carriers. Attack these one at a time with the full force of your air group and Dragoons and they should give you no trouble—but don't ignore them! If you don't take a pair of enemy Carriers seriously, they can ruin your day. Once you've destroyed the enemy (yellow) Nexus, you've won the scenario.

Resource Management

Initially you'll have sufficient raw resources at your disposal to meet your needs. Later on, however, you must seek a second source. It lies in the map's upper-middle portion. The enemy doesn't defend it heavily, but don't go after this mineral field until after you secure the center of the map.

Don't hesitate to build 20 Probes to harvest resources. The more you have working the faster the minerals and gas will come in, making it easier to mount an attack force before it dwindles in defending the base. Research to maximum levels;

you're facing off against other Protoss units, and if you haven't got an edge, you'll soon become a heap of twisted metal.

When your attack force is in place, keep producing Scouts, Zealots, and Dragoons. Use these units to form new groups of replacements for the casualties that mount as you attack enemy positions. The second base area is important for generating these backup units, because you'll use up your original resources building your attack force as you research new technologies.

MISSION #8:

The Trial of Tassadar

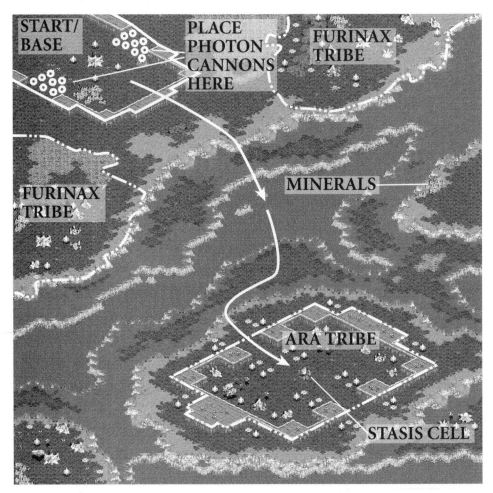

Fig. 6-27:

Map of Protoss Mission 8.

Mission Overview

Fenix believes that all is lost, but nonetheless insists you continue to fight onward to find Tassadar and release him from the Judicator before they can execute him for treason. Tassadar offers the only hope for unlocking the Dark Templar's powers to defeat the Zerg onslaught.

Zeratul and his Dark Templar have vanished, leaving the Protoss to fend for themselves in this dark hour. However, help has arrived from an unlikely source. Jim Raynor, the Terran, has offered to help find and rescue Tassadar because Tassadar helped him in the past. May luck be with you as you search for Tassadar in this dark hour.

Mission Objectives

* Destroy the Stasis Cell.
* Raynor and Fenix must survive.

Special Units

* Stasis Cell
* Fenix (Dragoon)
* Raynor (Battle Cruiser)

New Units

* Carrier

Battle Strategy

Your base lies in the upper left corner of the map and is mercifully contained by a large wall that has only two entrances/exits. This, however, is not nearly enough to protect you from the constant attacks during this mission. Therefore, you should place Photon Cannons in bunches (at least six) at the entrance/exits of your base. This may sound excessive, but a group of six Photon Cannons probably can't hold off the attacks so put a fully loaded Carrier at each entrance as well.

Fig. 6-28:

This may seem like overkill, but you'll need large groups of Photon Cannons to stem the tide of enemy attacks.

Obviously, this mission will involve some hunkering down to defend the base while you build up your forces to the point that you can make an effective strike at the Stasis Cell. The Stasis Cell lies roughly in the central-lower portion of the map, and is on a somewhat isolated island that's defended by the Ara Tribe. The best way to reach the Stasis Cell is to move two groups of Carriers and Scouts in from the air, with Raynor in his Battlecruiser as backup.

Counterpoint

If you long for ground combat, you can reach the Stasis Cell along the ground by following the water's edge along the right hand edge of the map, but we don't recommend it. To take this path you'd have to pass by one of the Furinax Tribe's bases, and considering your limited resources, it will be tough to fight through two bases without losing even a large attack force. Using a small ground force as a decoy is probably a better plan if you're chomping at the bit for ground combat.

Fig. 6-29:

The enemy will be eager to use the Stasis Field ability on your units, so try to keep your groups far enough apart that not all of your units will get frozen.

The enemy will continually launch attacks at the two openings in your bases' walls, but don't waste too many resources on these defenses or you won't be able to assemble an attack fleet. Keep building Photon Cannons to replace any that are destroyed, and build Zealots as backup.

Once you have four fully loaded Carriers and six to eight Scouts, group them into two equal units and fly toward the Stasis Cell. Take care not to get too close to the Ara Tribe bases along the way (see figure 6-27). When you get to the island that houses the Stasis Cell, be prepared for some hot-and-heavy action, including getting put into Stasis by an enemy Arbiter. If this happens, the "stasised" units cannot be harmed, but they also cannot move or attack effectively, and so become temporarily useless. Keeping your attacking units physically distant from each other is your best defense against a Stasis attack, so we recommend using two smaller groups of ships in this scenario.

 Stasis

At first glance, the Arbiter's Stasis ability may not seem to serve much of a purpose, however there's one very good reason to use it. If half of an attacking group of enemy units is in Stasis, than you have effectively removed half of the attackers, making it easier to take out the remaining units. When the Stasis field wears off, you'll have already killed off half the enemy units, greatly reducing the attack forces effectiveness.

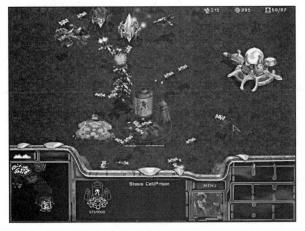

Fig. 6-30:

Don't worry about the other structures near the Stasis Cell, just make a run for it and shoot at it with everything you've got.

When you hit the island, all of the Photon Cannons, Scouts, Dragoons, Carriers, and Arbiters giving you their undivided attention may prove distracting. But, any attempt to clear out all the enemy units will only result in failure, so you should move straight for the Stasis Cell and attack hard. If you're having trouble punching through to the Cell, divert the enemy units with one group of Scouts while your Carriers make their move on the Cell. The Stasis Cell falls quickly under heavy fire, so being aggressive can bring you victory.

Resource Management

The limiting factors in this scenario are Vespene Gas, and, to a lesser extent, minerals. Although resources can get tight near the end of the mission, there are certainly enough to support your defenses as you build up a solid strike force capable of punching through the Ara Tribe's defense.

To prevent unnecessary resource drains due to heavy defensive losses, build up a large number of Photon Cannons right away. It may seem like a waste of resources, but the enemy attacks in large waves and only groups of six to ten Photon Cannons on each exit will stem the tide. Keeping some Zealots and later, a Carrier at each exit will help to keep your expensive buildings safe as you research the tech tree.

When you run out of resources around your base, you won't be able to get resources from enemy positions. The one resource area left is fairly distant from your starting location (see figure 6-27). Therefore, watch your resources carefully and try not to get into any shooting matches where you must battle it out with tons of enemy units. If this happens, you'll probably lose.

MISSION #9:
SHADOW HUNTERS

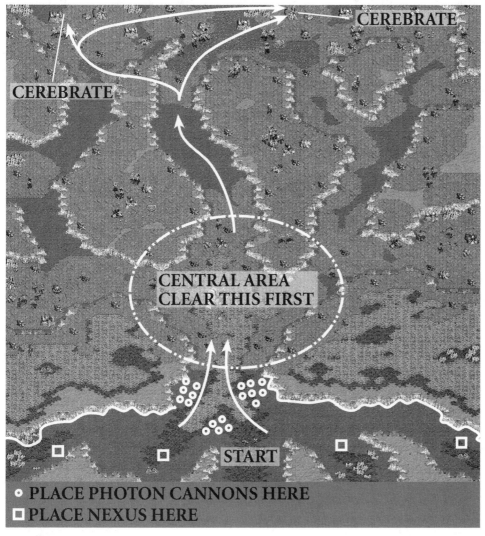

Fig. 6-31:
Map of Protoss Mission 9.

Mission Overview

Now that Tassadar and Zeratul are free, Zeratul reveals that he contacted the essence of the Overmind when he slew the Cerebrate on Char. Zeratul's mind was filled with the Overmind's thoughts and now knows that the Zerg have come not only to conquer the Protoss, but also to conquer the galaxy!

Fenix will engage the primary Zerg Hive clusters in an attempt to weaken their defenses. Once the Zerg numbers are thinned, Zeratul and his companions can infiltrate the clusters and assassinate the Cerebrates.

Mission Objectives

* Use Zeratul to destroy the Zerg Cerebrates.
* Zeratul and Fenix must survive.

Special Units

* Zeratul
* Fenix (in Dragoon)

New Units

* Arbiter

Battle Strategy

You begin with a small contingent of units that includes Fenix and Zeratul. You also have some Probes you need to put to use building several Nexii in the mineral fields near your starting point (see figure 6-31). You must build up a grid of Photon Cannons in the central area of the map to take care of the Zerg that will flow frequently down from the north.

Fig. 6-32:

This may look excessive, but there's method in this madness. This defense grid will allow you to prepare your attack force in peace.

Build up a group of at least six Carriers and four Scouts, then add your Arbiter (which you start out with) and an Observer (which will let you see buried Zerg). After you build up all the structures you need and research the tech tree, building a fleet of Carriers complete with eight Interceptors in each won't be easy. You'll have to scrape together the resources if you want to do it in a timely manner. Send this attack north to clear out the lower-middle area of the map. Once this area is secured (and it'll take a while), park your Carriers at the mouth of the three pathways and use them to take out any Zerg units that come south.

Fig. 6-33:

Use your Carrier force to secure this central area. It won't be pretty; there's plenty of enemy units around.

You can now prepare for the final push. Start building Templars by the handful so that you can create a large group of Archons to compliment your air force. Once you have seven or eight Archons in place, move them up the central pathway along with eight or so Zealots and Zeratul. When you come to the first Cerebrate, clear out all the enemy units that threaten Zeratul. Then use Zeratul to kill the Cerebrate. If you need any extra support at this time, move your Carrier force up to clear out or distract any enemy units that are getting in your way. Move to the right along the top of the map to the last Cerebrate and repeat the death scene with Zeratul.

Fig. 6-34:

You must use Zeratul to kill the Cerebrate. Otherwise they just reincarnate.

TIP

Carriers and Arbiters

Take time in this mission to get a feel for using Carriers and Arbiters together. Anything within a certain radius of an Arbiter is cloaked, which takes sneak attacks to a whole new level of terror. To the enemy it looks as if only one ship is approaching (the Arbiter), but in fact the Arbiter may cloak as many as eight Carriers. Because the Arbiter is faster than the Carriers, it's a good idea to tell the Arbiter to "follow" by highlighting the Arbiter and right-clicking on one of the Carriers, thereby providing cloaking cover at all times.

Resource Management

Begin by using your initial minerals to build two Nexus structures near the two mineral fields at the bottom of the map (one in the lower-left corner and one in the lower-right area). You start with 1000 gas units, so you can wait a short time before building a Nexus near one of the geysers. Generally, the distances between the geysers and the mineral fields make it easier and more efficient for you to build a Nexus at every single resource source.

Once you've set up every Nexus, you should have three geysers and three mineral fields being harvested simultaneously (see figure 6-31). This may seem like overkill, but you'll need all these resources to punch a hole in the thick Zerg defense that guards the two Cerebrates. As soon as you've got all your income sources flowing, it will help you to build the structures you need to climb the tech tree quickly.

MISSION #10:
EYE OF THE STORM

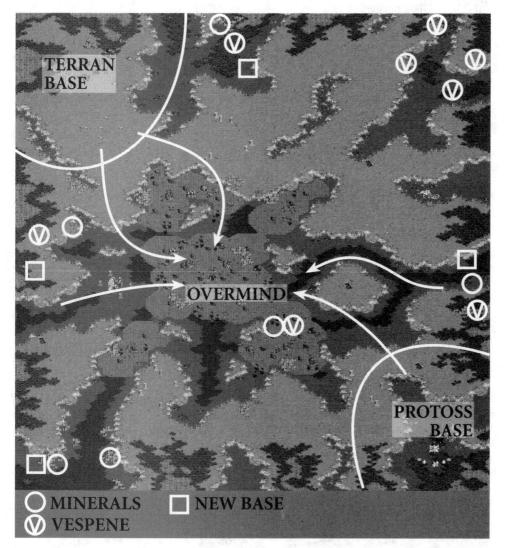

TERRAN
BASE

OVERMIND

PROTOSS
BASE

⭕ MINERALS   ⬜ NEW BASE
Ⓥ VESPENE

Fig. 6-35:
Map of Protoss Mission 10.

Mission Overview

Zerg defenses are broken and the path to the Overmind laid bare. The Overmind has come to destroy all the Protoss (and Terrans) hold dear and assimilate every being into itself. It's time to strike down the Overmind no matter the cost.

En Taro Adun, brave warriors!

Mission Objectives

* Destroy the Overmind.
* The Gantrithor (Tassadar), the Hyperion (Raynor), and Zeratul must survive.

Special Units

* Tassadar (in Carrier)
* Zeratul (Dark Templar)
* Raynor (in Battlecruiser)

New Enemy Unit (Zerg)

* Overmind

Battle Strategy

This mission is the game's greatest challenge, as it should be. It may take a few tries to get established enough for victory. You start with two bases under your control—one Protoss (in the lower-right corner) and one Terran (in the upper-left corner)—and you must cultivate and protect both against massive and unpredictable Zerg attacks.

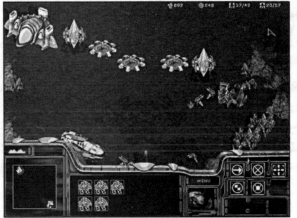

Fig. 6-36:

A line of Photon Cannons and some ground units should be enough to defend your Protoss base.

First, hotkey the Terran Command Center and the Protoss Nexus to keys **0** and **9**. This way you can jump quickly from base to base without having to scroll across the map. Managing two bases is very important in this mission, and you'll probably end up with four or five before it's over.

 The Zerg will attack both your initial bases with Zerglings, Hydralisks, and Mutalisks (usually in separate large groups), so build up solid defenses. You may have to restart this level more than once if you underestimate the Zerg.

In the beginning, both of your bases are vulnerable to Zerg attack, so build up defenses in both locations if you want to survive the first half-hour of play. In the Terran base it's hard to beat a line of Bunkers filled with upgraded Marines, but you can be sure that the Zerg will throw a group of 12 Mutalisks at you, so build Missile Turrets or more Marine-filled Bunkers behind your front lines.

The Protoss have the Dark Templars and Tassadar as backup, but take care not to lose either Zeratul or Tassadar or the mission will end. However, these special units afford you an extra measure of protection while you set up a grid of Photon Cannons and build Zealots and Dragoons for defense.

Fig. 6-37:

You can attempt to fight your way to the Overmind using Siege Tanks and air suport but you'll be in for a tough time.

After moving out to harvest some of the extra resource pools scattered across the map, concentrate on upgrading all your units' abilities and technologies. As this is going on, build up a massive, balanced attack force comprising at least eight groups of 12 units each: Zealots (two groups), Dragoons (one group), Scouts (one group), Carriers (one group), Firebats (one group), Marines (one group), Wraiths (one group), and Battlecruisers (one group). If you like, assign your last hotkey to Dragoons. Hotkey all your groups to keys **1** through **9** and your Comsat Station to **0**.

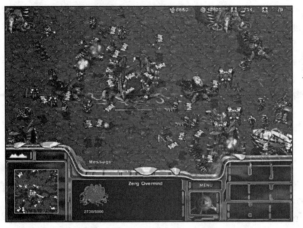

Fig. 6-38:

The Overmind's attack will be spectacular, and if you play your cards right, you'll win.

When all your groups are ready to fight (this will take a long time), you can defeat the Overmind using a simultaneous Terran-Protoss double-pronged attack. Using your Comsat Station, expose the Overmind. Then quickly move through your groups, telling each to attack the Overmind. All 100-plus units will make a run for the Overmind and attack in a flurry of Interceptors, acid sprays and bloodshed. If you've constructed your groups properly, the Overmind will die before the last of your units bites it.

 Keep a close eye on your special units (Tassadar, Zeratul, and Raynor) because if you lose one, the mission ends. It's all too easy to group Tassadar or Raynor with bunches of units being sent to their deaths near the Overmind, and if they die, you lose.

If you don't want to endure the final battle as all units converge on the Overmind, move against the Overmind's position slowly by inching Siege Tanks toward the objective. Zerg defenses are thick, however, and a long, slow battle may drain your resources before you get there. The large strike provides the spectacular conclusion a great game like *StarCraft* deserves.

Resource Management

This map is *StarCraft's* richest in resources, and you'll need them to reach the Overmind. Large mineral and Vespene stores lie around the perimeter (see figure 6-35), and you must get harvesting to build up the attack force you need to penetrate Zerg defenses.

After you've set up a solid network of Bunkers, Photon Cannons, Missile Turrets, and ground units to protect both initial bases, your resources probably will be substantially reduced. Because your main bases are well-protected, move some SCVs and Probes to new mineral and Vespene areas. The Zerg don't defend the new areas directly, but periodic Zerg patrols sweep the area, so keep some protective units on hand while you set up new Command Centers and Nexuses.

In this scenario it's important to build up a huge attack force before making your move, so try to exploit every free mineral and Vespene area on the map. When you've banked 10,000 minerals, you may be tempted to take a run at the Overmind, but you really should wait until you've assigned every hotkey a group of 12 units.

Expand to the areas on the map's central right-hand edge, central left-hand edge, and lower-left corner first. Do this fairly rapidly (using air units for mobile defense), and you'll amass your attack troops quickly.

If you're short on Vespene, the four geysers in the map's upper-right corner contain enough Vespene to make anyone happy. One Nexus or Command Center can sit amid the four vents and receive a constant stream.

Chapter 7:

MULTIPLAYER
GAMES

BATTLE.NET

To use Blizzard's free multiplayer service you must have a connection to the Internet. If you have a dial-up account that uses a modem to connect to the Internet, make sure you connect successfully before starting *StarCraft*. This saves time and frustration, especially if you must troubleshoot problems.

From the main *StarCraft* screen, select Multiplayer and then Battle.net. A message will indicate the game is searching for the fastest server; then you'll see the login screen. To create a new account, follow the onscreen instructions; otherwise, enter the user name and password for your existing account. Once you're logged on, you'll find yourself in one of many chat rooms.

Fig. 7-01:

Battle.net is a great way to make the fun of playing StarCraft last forever.

In the chat room you can meet friends for a prearranged game or find other players to battle. To join a game, hit the Join button and pick a game from the list, or type the name and password of a game you've previously agreed on with friends. To create a game, hit the Create button and type in a game name and password (optional). Using a password restricts entry to your game to those players who know the password. If you create a game, you may select the number of players, their species, and the map you'll play on.

Updates

Periodically, Blizzard updates its game software. When you sign onto Battle.net, the network determines whether you need to upgrade and, if you do, it automatically sends you the newer version of the game. After the new software is downloaded, the game restarts on its own and applies the upgrade. You must have the most recent version of *StarCraft* to play games on Battle.net.

Troubleshooting

The Internet can be a great way to play games interactively, but it can be like trying to communicate by using tin cans and a string. If you have problems getting *StarCraft* to work on Battle.net, keep these points in mind:

1. You must have a 32-bit connection to the Internet. It's difficult to know whether your connection is a true 32-bit link, but if you have any doubt, just remember that most connections are 32-bit connections.

    ✳ If you use Dial-Up Networking to connect, you most likely are getting a 32-bit connection.

    ✳ If, however, you use a terminal program or third-party dialer, you'll probably get only a 16-bit connection and be unable to play *StarCraft* on Battle.net.

    ✳ If you play other games on the Internet, you'll probably have no trouble with *StarCraft*.

2. The reason you need a 32-bit connection is because the game uses UDPs (Universal Datagram Packets) to send game information back and forth while you play. If your ISP(Internet service provider) doesn't allow these types of packets through, you won't be able to play on Battle.net. This is important to know if you use an account at your place of business or educational institution; often these types of ISP don't allow such game packets through.

3. If your connection is too slow, your game will be jumpy and unreliable. Your modem's (or other connection method's) line speed together with Internet conditions determine the speed of your connection.

Is the Connection Good?

Latency is a major factor in online gaming. In simple terms, latency is a measure of how long it takes your computer to communicate with the host computer that's running the game. Low latency is good, because it means the two computers communicate quickly. High latency is bad, because it means there's a significant delay between the events happening on the host computer and what you're actually seeing on your screen.

Once in Battle.net chat room, the latency bar next to your name shows your latency to Battle.net. In the list of games to join, your latency bar shows your latency to each game, which may be different than your latency to Battle.net. Short green bars mean you have very little latency. Longer yellow or red bars mean you've got significant latency.

The Multiplayer Experience

Multiplayer gaming differs significantly from single-player. For one thing, single-player missions are "set" while multiplayer affairs are like stories yet to be written. For another, human opponents provide an entirely different kind of gaming experience.

Multiplayer gaming also has more of an element of surprise, especially when you're playing with three or more opponents. Will your allies turn on you? Will your closest enemy ally with another player to crush you? The permutations that can occur in multiplayer games is mind-boggling, making multiplayer gaming the "spice" that keeps *StarCraft* interesting.

The Human Factor

Humans provide a much deeper and more challenging opponent than even the best computer AI. The rewards of playing against humans are many, and will make you a better *StarCraft* player, greatly improving your strategy skills.

What makes multiplayer action so much better? There are a few theories about that.

The Brain

Sure, Deep Blue can mentally outmuscle Gary Kasparov at chess, but those of us with everyday PCs on our desks don't have much to worry about. The human brain is still far and away the superior thinker when pitted against gaming AI. *StarCraft*'s AI is excellent, but once you know how to defeat a scenario, that's the end. However, when a human's at the enemy controls, you have no idea what will happen next. A human is a smart and unpredictable being, and that's what makes him or her such a great adversary.

Sure, you may understand human tendencies—they like to build 35 Siege Tanks, for example—but in the end, you never really know what a human will do.

The Grudge

Losing to a human usually makes you feel worse than losing to a computer. The resulting grudge will inspire you to try harder the next time you face off. Many of this book's best strategies came from two humans bashing on each other in a multiplayer game of *StarCraft*.

Gloating

The feeling of pride you get from defeating your friends can be a big motivator for improving your gaming skills. The satisfaction that comes from winning a multiplayer *StarCraft* game ranks much higher than kicking the computer's AI.

Taunting

For many, defeating a human usually means a chance to *rub it in.* Sure, it's juvenile, but taunting your enemies can throw off their game. Although it can backfire, big talk from a player can inspire crippling doubt in his or her opponent. If you get a message that says "I hope your flank's protected," does it mean that enemy is going to attack your flank? Is *another* player going to attack your flank? Or is he or she just messing around with your mind?

Multiplayer Tips

If you're new to the real-time strategy genre, or just want to brush up on your skills, consider the following helpful multiplayer tips.

Speed

The first thing you'll probably notice about human opponents is the speed with which they get their act in gear. You might still be tinkering with your base, defenseless, when suddenly a horde of enemies comes knocking on your door. This is especially common when your opponent(s) plays Zerg, because those cheap, easy-to-build Zerglings can cause havoc in the game's early stages.

Stay fast and focused during the first few minutes of your game. Build only the essentials and always keep an eye on defense. Don't build extraneous stuff until you've got a strong production chain and several combat units. And make sure you get lots of resource harvesters (such as SCVs) into action as quickly as possible. The more of them you have, the faster you can build your war machine.

Keep Your Scan Going

You should play *StarCraft* in a high energy state, always looking around the map for new areas to explore, new units to build, new resources to exploit, and new enemies to corner and kill. Never sit still to watch and wait for units to be completed or to reach their destinations. Time spent idly will cost you the game when you play against skilled opponents.

Establish a rhythm of scanning your units, building new ones, strengthening defenses, and mining new resources. Developing a methodical way of consistently reviewing your units can increase productivity and awareness considerably. Keep your mouse pointer busy.

Fig. 7-02:

Get in the habit of scanning your forces constantly.

For example, if you find a new area with resources to exploit, instead of waiting for new Drones to be built and move to the new area, send existing Drones now and have the new ones take over the old ones' activities. Also, don't let your buildings sit idle. If you're running too low on resources to build new units continually, increase the number of Drones/Probes/SCVs mining for minerals and gas (or find new sources of these resources).

Defending

Don't let your guard down. When you send a task force of soldiers to attack your enemy, keep some in reserve to defend your bases, and be sure to build a decent network of defensive structures. Clear-thinking players realize the best time to attack an enemy base is when the enemy is attacking yours. This forces the opponent to divide his or her attention and troops.

Establish a second and third base as soon as you can. If your opponent takes out your only base, the game is over. If your opponent finds an auxiliary base and destroys it, you're still in the game and can strike back.

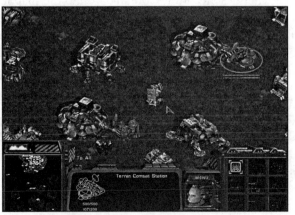

Fig. 7-03:

Getting multiple bases up and running is crucial to success in multiplayer games.

Having large numbers of cheap units is the most efficient way to wage war in the beginning and middle parts of the game, but once you've researched the tech tree fully you'll need to create more powerful defensive units. Don't neglect your research!

Attacking

Once you commit to an attack, *don't back down*. Keep producing and sending units to attack until you break the opposition. If it looks like you aren't making progress, don't give up! You'll win because most enemy players will be too preoccupied with defense to mount an attack of their own and come after you. Too often players attack with one or two waves of units and then give up, even though they're very close to breaking their enemies' backs.

It's helpful to build attacking units near your opponent's base. That way you can send reinforcements as soon as they're completed. *StarCraft*'s ability to queue up production and set "focal" (rally) points for units is a great aid for players mounting a sustained attack.

Fig. 7-04:

You may be tempted to create a "victory fleet" of 12 Battlecruisers or Carriers, but a balanced force often serves better.

Although it can be tempting to make a couple of large groups of your most powerful unit, this can be risky if your opponent knows how to counter that unit. Therefore, it's important to attack with at least two unit types. Include one unit type that can hit air targets and one that can hit ground units. This way your attack force can't be wiped out by one or two defenders it can't even touch.

As in real-life battle, your initial attack probably will be most effective if it comes from two or more directions at once. This forces the enemy to divide his defenders and attention while your forces pour in. Even if your other attacks are simply diversions, you'll force the enemy to defend against them all.

hapter 8:

CAMPAIGN EDITOR:
A WORLD
OF ITS OWN

O ne of the great things about StarCraft is that it ships with a campaign editor that allows you to create your own maps AND CREATE ENTIRE CAMPAIGNS, complete with story lines and characters. The only aspect of StarCraft the average person can't include in his or her own campaign is Blizzard's spectacular cutscenes.

It would take an entire book to convey how to manage and exploit every nuance of StarCraft's campaign editor! So it seemed best to go straight to the source— Blizzard—and have StarCraft tester Eric Dodds outline how to create a compelling map. Eric is largely responsible for the content that follows (with some help from Alen Lapidis), and I'm grateful for their contributions.

WHAT IS IT?

The *StarCraft* campaign editor is a complex tool that enables the user to create completely functional single-player and multiplayer maps, as well as campaigns (a series of maps where a story ties them together). Essentially, the editor is a user-friendly programming language that enables you to create new *StarCraft* realms.

The process of creating an entire campaign is very complex, and in the case of the development of *StarCraft*, the single-player version of the game required the skills of many individuals working together over a period of months. However, you don't have to spend months making a decent map or scenario that can be enjoyed over Battle.net or a home network.

Multiplayer Balancing

Perhaps the most important aspect of building a multiplayer map is to ensure that the map is balanced properly. By "balanced" we mean that the starting conditions for each player are relatively equal in resources, units, and terrain. If a game is unbalanced in this way, it will be discarded quickly unless one of the players is considerably better than the others. However, history shows that unbalanced maps die a quick death in the ring of public opinion.

Single-player Balancing

To balance a single-player map you must strive for a slightly different goal. A balanced single-player map makes the player use all of his or her abilities to win, but it isn't so difficult that winning is impossible. There's a fine line between creating a computer opponent that's too tough and one that's too wimpy. Creating a properly balanced map will provide a long, involved, and satisfying gaming experience for the player.

BUILDING YOUR OWN MAP

Before you start building a real map, try building a few simple maps to get a grasp of the basic aspects of map design (doodads, triggers, locations, and so on). This will save you time in the long run. Trying to make a complicated idea work before you've learned the ropes is never a good idea.

Remember, the map editor's online "Help" is *very* good. If you're confused, bring up online "Help" (press **F1**, or select "Help" from the Help menu) and you'll probably get the answer to your question.

To use all the cool triggers and locations, you must select the "Use Map Settings" game type when you start the game with the map. If you don't, you'll play on the terrain you've created, but with standard units, and none of your triggers or locations will work.

Steps for Building a Map

Here's one method for designing your own map. It's meant to be a basic walkthrough of some of the key components of map building, like placing "doodads" (little pieces of art) or "triggers" (linked events) throughout the map in hope of adding to the complexity and fun of the scenario you're trying to create. It should also be pointed out that creating a map can take days of work, and should not be approached as a one or two hour project. The following advice is far from a hard-and-fast road map, but it will help get you on course.

Some Definitions

TRIGGER: A trigger is something that "triggers" an event in the game. For example, if a player harvests more than 2000 gas units from a Vespene Geyser, you can tell the game to trigger ten Marines to spontaneously appear. There's probably no end to what you can make a trigger do, from causing enemy attacks to serving up a bit of story text.

DOODAD: Doodads are, for the most part, little bits of art like skeletons, signs or trees that are laid out around the map to add visual color. The only exception to this is ramps, which are also included in the doodad menu.

DESIGN THE MAP IN YOUR HEAD FIRST.

Come up with a basic idea before you sit down at the editor. Choose forces for each player and, more important, what special triggers you'll need to implement your idea. If you're experienced (or even if you aren't), go to the help screens for triggers (select "Help" from the menu, go to the index, and check out triggers) and see if what you want to do can be done.

Eric's Example of Trigger Use in "Gods of War"

I've decided on a scenario using three players. Each has a special power none of the others has. I want to call it "Gods of War" and create three special powers—one for each player—based on what I know about triggers and how they work.

The first player will have the ability to teleport around the map. I know the "moveto" trigger allows me to move units around the map. Player two will be a warrior type and will get hero units after a given number of kills. A "kill counter" enables the map to count kills, and I can make suitable hero units. The third player will be the "horde player," and will have lots of weak units. I'll set up the map so that if this player has the fewest units, a trigger will go off and he or she will receive free Zerglings until he or she no longer has the fewest units. This is made easy through the use of the "least" condition in the trigger menu.

SELECT THE TILESET.

The tileset is the basic pallet of terrain types you will want to use when creating your map. Select "New" from the "File" menu to pop up a dialogue box that asks for the base tileset you want. Browse through and select the tileset that best fits your idea. You'll also select your map's basic overall terrain type here. Not all terrain types can accept structures, so select fundamental terrain types for your first maps (dirt, jungle, grass, and the like).

NOTE

Eric's Tileset for "Gods of War"

The "Jungle" tileset best fits my idea for the "Gods of War" scenario and there are several doodads in this tileset I want in my map. I select "Jungle tileset" and then select "Jungle" for my basic terrain type, because that's how I want most of the map to look. I select a 128-by-128 tile map because I want the game to last just long enough to be interesting. This may be a little large for a three-player map, but 96-by-96 might be too small.

SET THE PLAYER SETTINGS.

To access this section, select "Players" from the menu bar and then select "Settings." The four main areas here allow you to play with the units and the tech tree.

Properties

This area controls race and whether a person, computer, group of rescuable units, or neutral player controls each unit. Choose settings appropriate for your scenario. For "Gods of War," Eric sets players one, two, and three on "Human." He sets players four through eight to "Neutral" because it's a three-player game with no computer players. Player one is Terran, player two Protoss, and player three Zerg. He ignores players four through eight; they won't be used.

Units

This area allows you to choose the units and structures each player has access to. For each player, you can select any unit and set it as unbuildable for that player. All players can build all units and buildings by default. If you want to keep a player from being able to build a specific unit or building, you can turn the units or buildings "off". You can also disable the global feature (which allows all players access to all units) by selecting a unit or building then removing the check box from the "Enabled by Default" box.

Upgrades

Set the starting level and maximum level each player can attain for each upgrade. Researchable upgrades have a setting of '0' if the upgrade isn't researched or '1' if it is.

Special Abilities

Here you select the special abilities each player starts with, from "disabled," "researched," or "enabled" (the default), for every special ability for each race. Eric's teleporting player will get "Recall" automatically, because teleportation is that player's theme.

SET FORCES.

Assign each player a force by clicking on the player's icon and dragging it to the force you want. You should also click on each force and name it to add a color (and help you remember which force does what when you assign triggers later).

NOTE Eric Sets the Forces

In the "Gods of War" scenario, I left player one in force one and named it "Warlord." I moved player two to force two and named it "Translocator." I moved player three to force three and named it "Master of the Horde." I moved the remaining players to the last force and left it nameless.

PLACE THE TERRAIN.

Go to the "Layer" menu and select "Terrain." A palette of the various terrain choices will come up. (Or you can click on the Terrain folder on the tool tree on the left side of the screen and select terrain types from a list.) Click on a selection in the palette or tool tree and paint the map with it, leaving room for units to move and to place resource areas.

PLACE THE RAMPS.

From the "Layer" menu, select "Doodads." At this point the only doodads we want to place are the ramps. The ramps can only be placed on the southeast or southwest angled cliffs (or walls) and can only be placed where the wall is flat and the ground is of the appropriate type for the specific ramp. Ramps are found in the cliff or wall doodad selection and are generally the last few doodads in their specific palette. The "Help" gives additional information about using the maps. Fire up "Help" and look up ramps in the index for more information on placing them.

PLACE THE UNITS.

Go to the layer menu and select the unit layer. In the tooltree menu on the left hand side is a list of players, and if you open the folder for a player it will have additional folders with types of units; ground units, air units, et cetera. Open one of these folders and click on the unit that you want to place on the map.

With each unit you place, you can double click on it to change the unit's properties. The properties you can change vary depending on the unit: For example, with Carriers and Reavers you can change how many Interceptors or Scarabs they start with. You can also change the percentage of hits a unit begins with as well as how much minerals or gas are contained within a mineral field or Vespene Geyser.

RESOURCES.

One of the first items that should be placed on the map is the resources; the Vespene Gas vents and mineral fields. Make sure you place enough mineral fields and gas vents at each starting location. It's also important to make sure there's enough room for each player to be able to establish a base in the starting area. In a standard game, each player starts with five or six mineral fields, containing 1500 minerals each, and a gas vent with 5000 gas.

The starting allocation of resources can be changed either by placing more of a resource type or by double-clicking on the resource and changing how many of that resource it provides. It's very important to place equal starting resources for each player because the initial resource allocation is a fairly important factor in balancing a scenario.

The resources each player receives at the start strongly influence the type of game that's played. Giving players very few starting mineral fields and vents forces them to expand to secondary towns early on. Giving them an abundance of gas vents and mineral fields allows them to camp and use their starting towns for their resource supplies for most of the game.

CHOOSE A STARTING LOCATION.

Select a starting location for each player using a special marker "unit." This tells the game where the player will start when the game begins. Place some of that player's starting units near the starting location; otherwise, when the game starts the player will see only a black screen area. Each player must have a starting location before you can save the game (and certainly before you can run it).

PLACE STRUCTURES.

Next, place each player's structures. Typically this means placing a Command Center, Nexus, or Hatchery on or near the starting location for each player. Then place the other structures as your design requires.

Each player starts with a town hall (Command Center, Nexus, or Hatchery) and a structure that provides additional supplies (Pylon, Supply Depot, or Overlord). This allows each player to concentrate on building various units instead of wasting resources by building supply units.

PLACE SPECIAL ITEMS.

"Special" is for things like the Terran player's Beacons, Flags, and Spider Mines. Beacons are useful for marking special locations. (See the "Create locations" section later in this chapter for details.)

 Eric's "Special" Placement

I need a number of special Beacons in "Gods of War." The Protoss player needs four to tell that player where his or her four teleport "locations" are. The Terran player needs a Beacon to mark where heroes will appear when his or her kills earn them. The Zerg player's Beacon will indicate where needed Zerglings will appear.

PLACE STARTING UNITS.

Next, place each player's starting units. A standard start provides each player with a few basic harvesting units. Add other units as your design dictates, but remember— you probably shouldn't start players with more units than their Psi/supplies/command rating will support. That is, start your players with enough Supply Depots, Pylons, or Overlords to support their starting units.

CREATE LOCATIONS.

Locations are special map areas directly tied to triggers. Because locations are invisible during gameplay, Beacons often are used to indicate location areas.

To create a location, select the "Layer" menu option and go to "Locations." At this point, you'll create a location anywhere you click on the map. Create a small location; click on the map's corner boxes, holding the mouse button down as you move it to change the location's size. When the location is the size you want it, click on the center of the location and hold down the mouse button to drag it to where you want it to be. Double-click on the location to change its name. Naming locations to reflect their functions makes it easier to select them when you assign triggers than trying to remember if you want location 7, 8, or 9. Locations will make more sense after you've played with triggers a little bit.

ASSIGN TRIGGERS.

Triggers are the campaign editor's heart and soul. They're what make it so powerful. Triggers are a limited scripting language that allow you to have game events occur in response to the actions of one or more players.

To create a new trigger, select the "Scenarios" menu option and then select "Triggers." A large dialogue box will come up listing default triggers. These control when a player wins or loses, and how much minerals and gas a player starts with.

Click on the "New" button for a list of players. Select the players you want the new trigger to affect, and then click "Next" to create the conditions that will set the trigger off.

Click on "New" to create a new conditional. (Use online "Help" to learn what each conditional does.) You must create at least one conditional to continue to the next screen. Choose from among a pull-down list of conditional templates. When you select a conditional, a statement will appear in the box below the list. Click on highlighted words to make the conditional work in your specific instance. The highlighted area will allow you to select what type of unit you want to test for, or which location the player must arrive at to set off the conditional. You can make it so a player must meet more than one conditional to activate a trigger.

After creating all the trigger conditionals you want, click on "Next" to set up the action(s) that take place when they're met. These appear in the same format as conditionals. Actions are things that will happen after a player meets your conditions. Typical actions are "Player gets 100 mineral units" or "Create a Marine for the player at a certain location." Select your actions the way you selected your conditionals.

When you're done with actions, you've created a trigger.

Triggers for "Gods of War"

TERRAN WHO GETS HEROES FOR KILLS

PLAYER: one

CONDITION: if player one kills x units

ACTION: create unit "Hero Y" at location "Terran hero arrival area"

PROTOSS TRANSPORT LOCATIONS

PLAYER: two

CONDITION: if player two brings a unit to location "teleporter x"

ACTION: move all units at location "teleporter x" to location "teleporter x destination"

THE ZERG ZERGLING HORDE

PLAYER: three

CONDITION: if player three has the least amount of units

ACTION: create a Zergling at location "Zergling arrival area"

ADD DOODADS.

Doodads are the little bits of art that spice up your map, make it look interesting, give it flavor. Select "Doodads" from the "Layers" menu to bring up a doodad palette. To place a doodad, select a terrain type from the pull-down menu bar at the top of the palette. Move the slider bar next to the doodad icon up and down to scroll through the doodads. Click on the doodad you want and click on the map to place it.

Some doodads are flat and units can walk over them; others *aren't* flat and units must walk around them. Which is which can be obvious, but sometimes you must figure it out on your own. Note, too, that trees affect combat. A unit in the trees has only a 70 percent chance of taking a hit, so placing trees can create interesting strategic possibilities.

CREATE A MISSION BRIEFING.

Focus your briefings, either toward *you*, the player, or between the characters in the portraits. A built-in "transmission" trigger is specifically designed to time portrait talking time and text displayed to the length of the audio track (.wav file) so both are presented fluently. Alternatively, you can display only a talking portrait and text. Remember that .wav files increase a map file's size, and usually briefing .wavs are largest. To display text-based dialog, use the following trigger order:

Portrait Slot# ON

{

Talking Portrait Slot #

Display Text

Wait

}

You want to keep the portraits open until the end of a conversation, so you'll probably want to hold off on disabling slots until the end of the conversation to keep it flowing smoothly. Make sure talking time, text time, and wait time all match. You may need to toy around with timing a bit to present the effect you want.

A good practice is to present players with mission objectives first, so the lower-left corner isn't left empty and so they don't miss the goals.

End the briefing with a one-line statement that the briefing is over, and then turn all port slots off.

EXPERIMENT!

All this gives you a brief look into the complex workings of the campaign editor. But this is only a small sampling of what you can do using this tool. To become an expert, *experiment,* use the online "Help," look at how triggers are used in other maps, and don't stop until you've made the kick-butt scenario or campaign of all time!

Appendices

A: Unit Tables
B: Tech Trees
C: Cheat Codes

Fig. A-1:

Terran Unit Table

Unit	Armor Type	Supply	Vespene Gas	Mineral	Hit Points	Ground Attack Strength	Air Attack Strength	Cooldown Rate	Biological Unit	Detector	Attack Range
Battlecruiser	Heavy	8	300	400	500	25E	25E	50	—	—	6/10
Dropship	Heavy	2	100	100	150	0	0	0	—	—	0
Firebat	Light	1	25	50	50	16PS	0	37	X	—	2
Ghost	Light	1	75	25	45	10P	10P	37	X	—	6
Goliath	Heavy	2	50	100	125	10	20E	37	—	—	5
Marine	Light	1	0	50	40	6	6	25	X	—	4
Missile Turret	Heavy	0	0	100	200	0	20E	25	—	X	7
Science Vessel	Heavy	2	300	25	200	0	0	0	—	—	8
SCV	Light	1	0	50	60	5	0	25	X	—	1
Siege Tank—Siege	Heavy	2	100	150	150	70ES	0	125	—	—	12
Siege Tank—Tank	Heavy	2	100	150	150	30E	0	62	—	—	6
Vulture	Medium	2	0	75	80	20P	0	50	—	—	5
Wraith	Heavy	2	100	200	120	8	15E	37	—	—	5

Key

S = Splash damage

P = Damage is reduced to attacking 50% when attacking Medium armor and 25% when attacking Heavy armor.

E = Indicates explosion attack (50% damage to Light Armor 75% damage to Medium Armor)

Cooldown = Time between attacks

Units that are in the trees when attacked only have a 70% chance of being hit.
Units attacking high ground from low ground only have a 70% chance to hit.

Fig. A-2:

ZERG UNIT TABLE

Unit	Armor Type	Supply	Vespene Gas	Mineral	Hit Points	Ground Attack Strength	Air Attack Strength	Cooldown Rate	Biological Unit	Detector	Attack Range
Broodling	Light	1	0	0	30	4	0	25	X	—	0
Defiler	Medium	2	100	25	80	0	0	0	X	—	4
Drone	Light	1	0	50	40	5	0	37	X	—	4
Egg	Heavy	0	0	1	200	0	0	0	X	—	0
Guardian	Heavy	2	100	50	150	20	0	50	X	—	8
Hydralisk	Medium	1	25	75	80	10E	10E	25	X	—	5
Infested Terran	Light	1	50	100	60	500	0	50	X	—	1
Larva	Light	0	0	1	25	0	0	0	X	—	0
Mutalisk	Light	2	100	100	120	9	9	37	X	—	3
Overlord	Heavy	-7	0	100	200	0	0	0	X	X	0
Queen	Medium	2	150	100	120	0	0	0	X	—	0
Scourge	Light	.5	75	25	20	0	110	50	X	—	1
Spore Colony	Heavy	0	0	50	400	0	15E	25	—	X	7
Sunken Colony	Heavy	0	0	75	400	30E	0	37	—	—	7
Ultralisk	Heavy	6	200	200	400	20	0	25	X	—	1
Zergling	Light	.5	0 .	50	35	5	0	15	X	—	0

Key

S = Splash damage

P = Damage is reduced to attacking 50% when attacking Medium armor and 25% when attacking Heavy armor.

E = Indicates explosion attack (50% damage to Light Armor 75% damage to Medium Armor)

Cooldown = Time between attacks

Units that are in the trees when attacked only have a 70% chance of being hit.
Units attacking high ground from low ground only have a 70% chance to hit.

Fig. A-3:

PROTOSS UNIT TABLE

Unit	Armor Type	Supply	Vespene Gas	Mineral	Shield	Hit Points	Ground Attack Strength	Air Attack Strength	Cooldown Rate	Biological Unit	Detector	Attack Range
Arbiter	Heavy	4	500	25	150	200	10E	10E	75	—	—	5
Archon	Heavy	4	300	100	350	10	30	30	25	—	—	3
Carrier	Heavy	8	300	350	150	250	5	5	4	—	—	8
Dragoon	Heavy	2	50	150	80	100	20E	20E	50	—	—	4
High Templar	Light	2	150	50	40	40	0	0	50	X	—	3
Observer	Light	1	75	25	20	40	0	0	0	—	X	0
Photon Cannon	Heavy	0	0	150	100	100	20E	20E	37	—	X	7
Probe	Light	1	0	50	20	20	5	0	37	—	—	1
Reaver	Heavy	4	100	200	80	100	100ES	0	50	—	—	8
Scout	Heavy	2	100	300	90	130	8	24E	37	—	—	4
Shuttle	Heavy	2	0	200	60	80	0	0	0	—	—	0
Zealot	Light	2	0	100	80	80	16	0	37	X	—	1

Key

S = Splash damage

P = Damage is reduced to attacking 50% when attacking Medium armor and 25% when attacking Heavy armor.

E = Indicates explosion attack (50% damage to Light Armor 75% damage to Medium Armor)

Cooldown = Time between attacks

Units that are in the trees when attacked only have a 70% chance of being hit.

**Units attacking high ground from low ground only have a 70% chance to hit.*

Fig. A-4:

TERRAN STRUCTURES

Terran Structure	Armor	Gas Needed to Build	Minerals Needed to Build	Shield	Hit Points	Build Time
Command Center	Heavy	0	400	0	1500	120
Supply Depot	Heavy	0	100	0	500	40
Refinery	Heavy	0	100	0	750	40
Barracks	Heavy	0	150	0	1000	80
Engineering Bay	Heavy	0	125	0	850	60
Academy	Heavy	0	200	0	600	80
Bunker	Heavy	0	100	0	350	30
Factory	Heavy	100	200	0	1250	80
Armory	Heavy	50	100	0	750	80
Starport	Heavy	100	200	0	1300	80
Science Facility	Heavy	200	150	0	850	80
Machine Shop	Heavy	50	50	0	750	40
Control Tower	Heavy	50	100	0	500	40
Physics Lab	Heavy	50	50	0	600	40
Covert Operations	Heavy	50	50	0	750	40
Nuclear Silo	Heavy	100	100	0	600	80
Comsat Station	Heavy	50	50	0	500	40

Fig. A-5:

ZERG STRUCTURES

Zerg Structure	Armor	Gas Needed to Build	Minerals Needed to Build	Shield	Hit Points	Build Time
Hatchery	Heavy	0	300	0	1250	100
Creep Colony	Heavy	0	75	0	400	20
Extractor	Heavy	0	50	0	750	40
Spawning Pool	Heavy	0	150	0	750	80
Evolution Chamber	Heavy	0	75	0	750	40
Hydralisk Den	Heavy	50	100	0	850	40
Spire	Heavy	150	200	0	600	120
Queen's Nest	Heavy	100	150	0	850	60
Nydus Canal	Heavy	0	150	0	250	40
Ultralisk Cavern	Heavy	200	150	0	600	80
Defiler Mound	Heavy	100	100	0	850	60
Greater Spire	Heavy	150	100	0	1000	80
Lair	Heavy	100	150	0	1800	100
Hive	Heavy	150	200	0	2500	120

Fig. A-6:

PROTOSS STRUCTURES

Protoss Structure	Armor	Gas Needed to Build	Minerals Needed to Build	Shield	Hit Points	Build Time
Gateway	Heavy	0	150	500	500	60
Forge	Heavy	0	200	550	550	40
Cybernetics	Heavy	0	200	500	500	60
Shield Battery	Heavy	0	100	200	200	30
Robotics Facility	Heavy	200	200	500	500	60
Stargate	Heavy	200	200	600	600	80
Citadel of Adun	Heavy	100	200	450	450	60
Robotics Support Bay	Heavy	100	50	450	450	30
Observatory	Heavy	100	150	250	250	60
Fleet Beacon	Heavy	200	300	500	500	60
Templar Archives	Heavy	200	100	500	500	60
Arbiter Tribunal	Heavy	150	200	500	500	60
Nexus	Heavy	0	400	750	750	120
Pylon	Light	0	100	300	300	30
Assimilator	Heavy	0	100	450	450	40

Fig. A-7:

HERO STATISTICS

Hero	Armor Type	Armor	Shield	Hit Points	Ground Attack Strength	Air Attack Strength	Cooldown Rate	Range
Raynor (Marine)	Light	3	0	200	18	18	25	4
Raynor (Vulture)	Medium	3	0	300	30P	30P	50	5
Norad II	Heavy	4	0	700	50	50	50	6
Zeratul	Light	0	400	60	100	—	—	1
Fenix (Zealot)	Light	2	240	240	40	0	37	1
Fenix (Dragoon)	Heavy	3	240	240	45E	45E	50	4
Tassadar	Light	2	300	80	20	0	50	3
Gantrithor	Heavy	3	500	800	0	0	—	8
Hunter Killer	Medium	2	0	160	20E	20E	25	5
Infested Kerrigan	Light	2	0	400	50	0	—	1
Dark Templar	Light	0	80	40	45	0	—	—
Kerrigan	Light	3	0	250	30P	30P	37	6
Raynor (Battlecruiser)	Heavy	4	0	700	30	30	50	6

Fig. A-8:

TERRAN COUNTER TABLE

A "Counter" is a unit that is best suited to match up against a particular unit in battle.

Unit	Zerg Counter	Protoss Counter	Terran Counter
Battlecruiser	Scourge	Scout	Goliath
Dropship	Mutalisk	Scout	Wraith
Firebat	Sunken Colony	Photon Cannon	Bunker
Ghost	Overlord	Observer	Scanner Sweep
Goliath	Queen Broodling	Zealot	Siege Tank
Marine	Zergling	Zealot	Firebat
Science Vessel	Scourge	Scout	Wraith
SCV	Zergling	Zealot	Marine
Siege Tank (Siege mode)	Queen Broodling	Templar Psi Storm	Wraith
Siege Tank (Tank)	Queen Broodling	Zealot	Wraith
Vulture	Hydralisk	Dragoon	Siege Tank
Wraith	Queen (Ensnare and Parasite)	Scout	Sensor Sweep

Fig. A-9:

Zerg Counter Table

A "Counter" is a unit that is best suited to match up against a particular unit in battle.

Unit	Zerg Counter	Protoss Counter	Terran Counter
Defiler	Ultralisk	Archon	Science Vessel (Irradiate)
Drone	Zergling	Zealot	Marine
Guardian	Scourge	Scout	Wraith
Hydralisk	Zergling	Zealot	Marine
Infested Terran	Zergling	Scout	Wraith
Mutalisk	Hydralisk	Scout	Goliath
Overlord	Hydralisk	Scout	Wraith
Queen	Scourge	Scout	Wraith
Scourge	Hydralisk	Dragoon	Goliath
Ultralisk	Guardian	Zealot	Battlecruiser
Zergling	Zergling	Zealot	Firebat

Fig. A-10:

PROTOSS COUNTER TABLE

A "Counter" is a unit that is best suited to match up against a particular unit in battle.

Unit	Zerg Counter	Protoss Counter	Terran Counter
Arbiter	Queen-Ensnare	Observer	Sensor Sweep
Archon	Zergling	Zealot	Science Vessel
Carrier	Scourge	Scout	Cloaked Wraith
Dragoon	Hydralisk	Zealot	Marine
High Templar	Queen Broodling	None	Science Vessel (Irradiate)
Observer	Spore Colony	Photon Cannon	Missile Turret
Probe	Zergling	Zealot	Marine
Reaver	Mutalisk	Scout	Wraith
Scout	Hydralisk	Dragoon	Goliath
Shuttle	Mutalisk	Scout	Wraith
Zealot	Zergling	Zealot	Firebat

Fig. B-1:

Terran Unit Dependencies

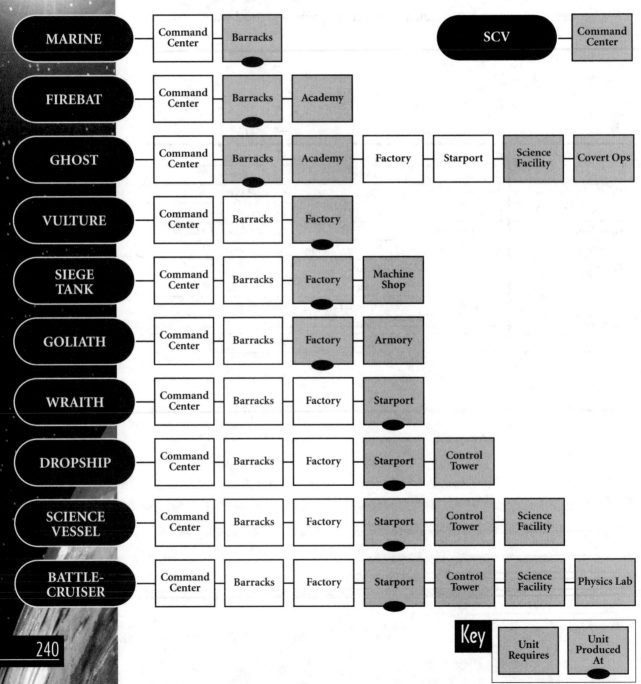

MARINE — Command Center — Barracks

FIREBAT — Command Center — Barracks — Academy

GHOST — Command Center — Barracks — Academy — Factory — Starport — Science Facility — Covert Ops

VULTURE — Command Center — Barracks — Factory

SIEGE TANK — Command Center — Barracks — Factory — Machine Shop

GOLIATH — Command Center — Barracks — Factory — Armory

WRAITH — Command Center — Barracks — Factory — Starport

DROPSHIP — Command Center — Barracks — Factory — Starport — Control Tower

SCIENCE VESSEL — Command Center — Barracks — Factory — Starport — Control Tower — Science Facility

BATTLE-CRUISER — Command Center — Barracks — Factory — Starport — Control Tower — Science Facility — Physics Lab

SCV — Command Center

Key: Unit Requires | Unit Produced At

Fig. B-2:

Zerg Unit Dependencies

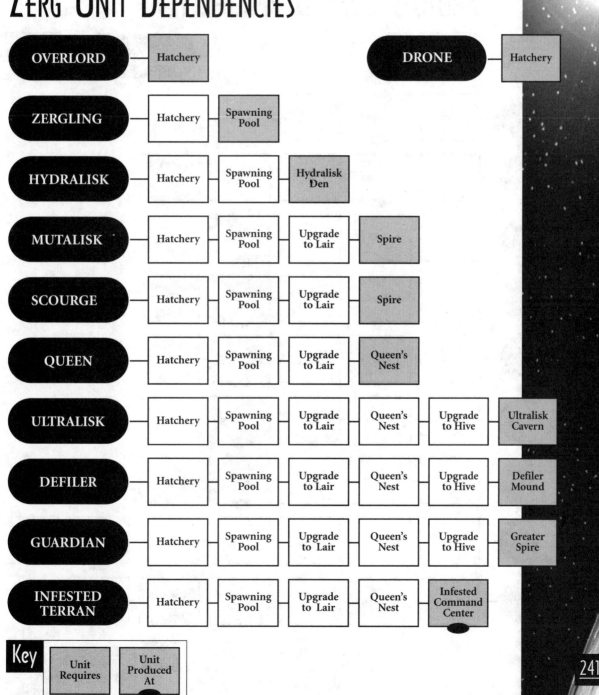

Key

| Unit Requires | Unit Produced At |

Fig. B-3:

PROTOSS UNIT DEPENDENCIES

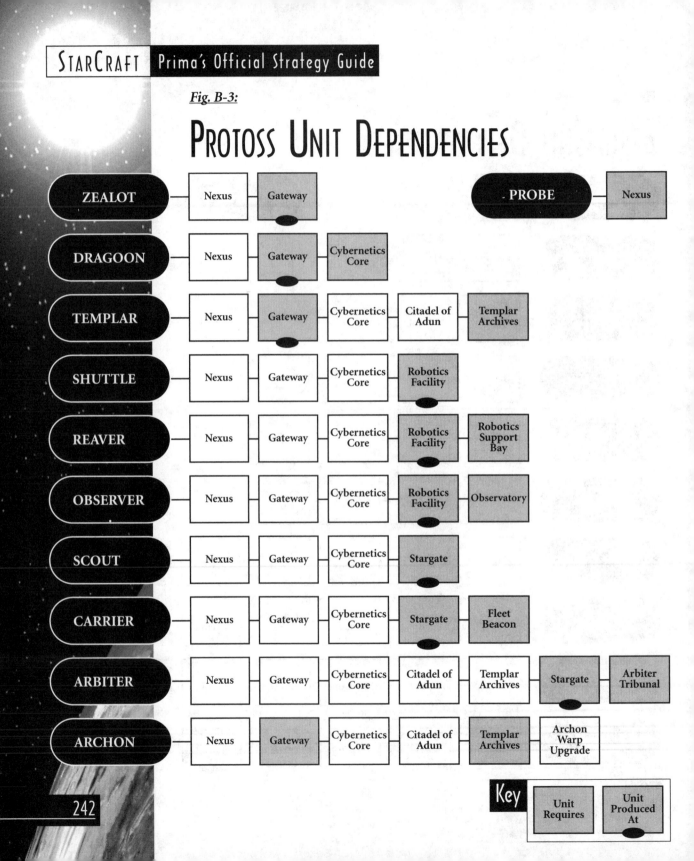

ZEALOT	Nexus	Gateway					
PROBE	Nexus						
DRAGOON	Nexus	Gateway	Cybernetics Core				
TEMPLAR	Nexus	Gateway	Cybernetics Core	Citadel of Adun	Templar Archives		
SHUTTLE	Nexus	Gateway	Cybernetics Core	Robotics Facility			
REAVER	Nexus	Gateway	Cybernetics Core	Robotics Facility	Robotics Support Bay		
OBSERVER	Nexus	Gateway	Cybernetics Core	Robotics Facility	Observatory		
SCOUT	Nexus	Gateway	Cybernetics Core	Stargate			
CARRIER	Nexus	Gateway	Cybernetics Core	Stargate	Fleet Beacon		
ARBITER	Nexus	Gateway	Cybernetics Core	Citadel of Adun	Templar Archives	Stargate	Arbiter Tribunal
ARCHON	Nexus	Gateway	Cybernetics Core	Citadel of Adun	Templar Archives	Archon Warp Upgrade	

Key

Unit Requires	Unit Produced At

Fig. B-4:

TERRAN BUILDING DEPENDENCIES

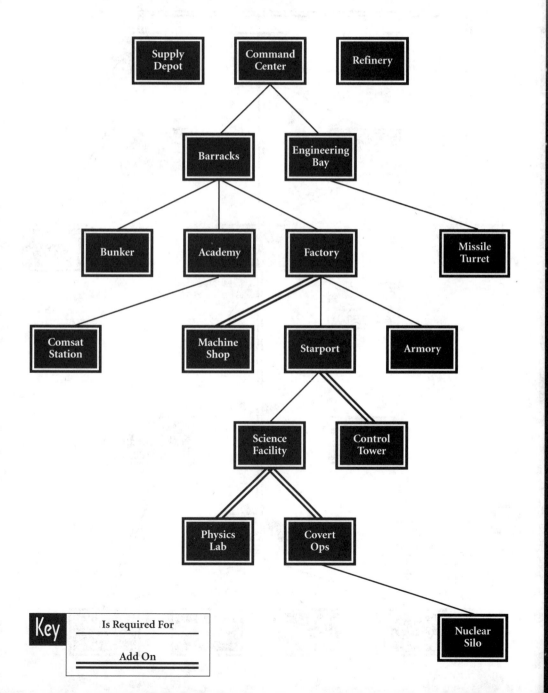

Supply Depot

Command Center

Refinery

Barracks

Engineering Bay

Bunker

Academy

Factory

Missile Turret

Comsat Station

Machine Shop

Starport

Armory

Science Facility

Control Tower

Physics Lab

Covert Ops

Nuclear Silo

Key

Is Required For
Add On

Fig. B-5:

ZERG BUILDING DEPENDENCIES

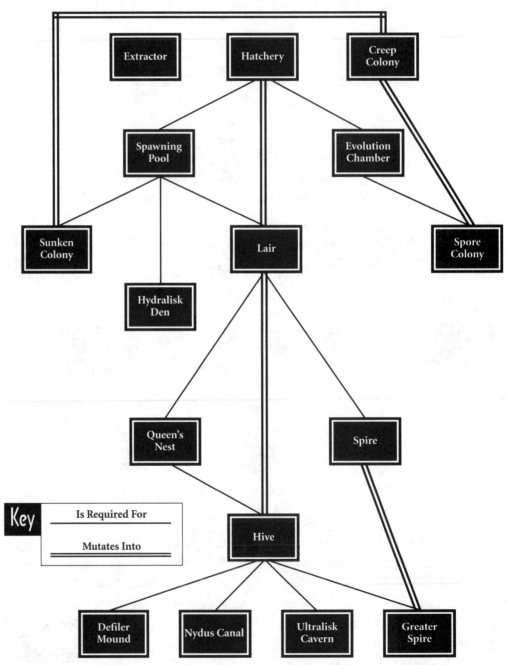

Key

Is Required For

Mutates Into

Fig. B-6:

PROTOSS BUILDING DEPENDENCIES

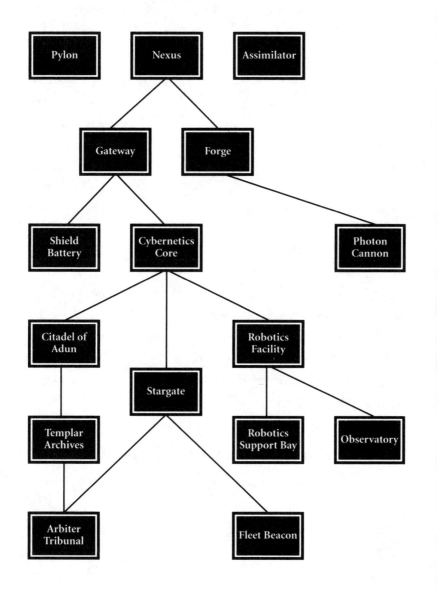

Fig. C-1:

CHEAT CODES

Once you've played all the way through *StarCraft*, you may wish to use the following cheat codes to enhance your experience of the game. These codes are not case sensitive, but be sure to include the spaces or they won't work. To enable these cheats, press Enter, type the cheat, and press Enter again.

Win the Mission	there is no cow level
Lose the Mission	game over man
God Mode	power overwhelming
Free Minerals and Vespene	show me the money
Free Minerals	whats mine is mine
Free Vespene	breathe deep
Gives All Available Upgrades	something for nothing
Show Entire Map	black sheep wall
Faster Building	operation cwal
Keep Playing After Victory	staying alive
Gives Units Free Upgrades	medieval man
Allows Any Structure to be Built	modify the phase variance
Disables Fog of War	war aint what it used to be
Build Units Beyond Supply Limit	food for thought
Use Special Abilities with No Energy Cost	the gathering
Skip to Any Mission	ophelia*

*Once you type "ophelia," press Enter. Then type the mission you wish to skip to.

NOTE Cheats only work in single player.